Marian

How to invest in stocks, bonds, commodities, and funds

Beginner Guide for all relevant asset classes focus on Europe

Imprint
© Copyright: 2023
MARISO AKADEMIE
Marian Sommer
Leo-Tolstoj-Str. 17K
60437 Frankfurt am Main
Translation: Robyn and Bernd Radermacher

Bibliographic Information of the German National Library:
The German National Library lists this publication in the German National Bibliography; detailed bibliographic data are available online at http://dnb.d-nb.de

Table of Contents

Motivation 8

Is it even possible to understand the stock market?............. 12

Basic knowledge: Securities Accounts and Investment Funds 15

  Securities account.. 15

  Clearing account.. 17

  Fees.. 18

    The difference between branch bank and direct bank .. 19

    The securities identification number 20

  Investment funds - when others do the work for you 21

    The investment fund... 22

    Accumulating or distributing of dividends.................. 23

    Indices 24

  Target funds.. 25

    The launch 25

    The initial charge... 26

    The hard life of the fund manager - the hunt for alpha. 27

    The fund price calculation 28

    Risks 29

  ETF.. 32

    The indices 33

    The costs.. 34

    Risks 35

    Practical tips 35

What role your bank or insurance broker plays............ 36

Terms from the fund world 38

Long/Short - or simply the side..................................... 38

Value /Growth – Stock picking 40

Balanced fund... 43

Hedge funds and hedge 44

Total Return / Absolute Return 46

Absolute Return Funds... 46

Total Return Funds... 47

Sustainable / ESG / SRI... 47

Counterparty / Issuer 49

Issuer 49

Counterparty... 49

Similarities and differences 49

Asset classes - the investment objects 50

Shares 51

The public limited company... 51

The Initial Public Offering - Primary Market............... 53

The stock market - the secondary market...................... 53

The stock exchange price 54

What does the current share price tell?.......................... 55

The dividends 56

Bonds... 59

Fixed income, bonds, debt securities - so many terms . 59

The issue with the market interest rate 59

The risk premium 61

The bond price.. 62

Special forms of bonds 63

Practical tips 64

Commodities 65

Futures 65

Certificates / ETC 67

Swaps 69

Precious metals - suitability as an investment object ... 73

Energy / Industrial metals / Food 79

Non-renewable raw materials... 79

Renewable raw materials.. 79

Risks 80

Contango and backwardation 81

Forward curves 81

The roll loss and its effect 82

Money market, foreign currencies.................................... 88

Savings account, call money, time deposit................... 88

Money market funds... 89

Foreign exchange and the foreign interest rate................. 90

Real Estate, Ships, Media.. 91

Closed-end funds.. 91

Open funds 92

Alternatives - practical tips.. 92

Volatility.. 93

The option market 93

Risk premiums and their dependence on volatility 94

Use as an asset class: opportunities and risks............... 95

Potential paths to wealth.. 98

The goal... 98

Timing of payout 101

Amount of the payout.. 101

The building blocks required to reach the goal. 102

Timing 102

Investment objects... 104

Target funds... 105

Individual stocks.. 105

ETFs 106

What can happen during the investment phase 108

Specific fund events 110

Important remarks at the end.. 124

Glossary... 127

Marian Sommer bought his first share at the age of 17 and thus came into contact with the stock exchange for the first time. During his studies in economics, with a focus on investment banking, he was actively involved in an investment club at his university.

After his studies, he started his first job in the certificates department of an investment bank and later changed to portfolio management at a capital management company in Frankfurt. There, he works in a lead position responsible for the administration and implementation of investment strategies for hundreds of investment funds.

Motivation

What is the reason for holding this book in your hands? Is it because you want to venture into the world of the stock market? Maybe you have lost money with shares and are asking yourself why. Or perhaps it is because you do not want to leave your money in times of low interest rates doing nothing for you? Do you want to build up your wealth? You might want to speculate or do as your neighbour, who talks non-stop about fantastic profits on the stock market. Whatever your motivation is, with this book I will give you the basic knowledge for just that and even more. I call it the Basics of the Stock Market.

In mathematics, you can try to get by without the basics (after all, there are calculators), but if you do not know the simplest relations between the numbers, you will stumble again and again. Let me apply this to the stock market; stumbling means losing money, and nobody wants that for sure.

After basic knowledge comes experience. This experience you need to build up yourself. However, I can help you avoid the first (expensive) mistakes when applying your knowledge.

Often, as an icebreaker at training courses for advanced stock exchange participants, the participants are asked the following questions: What was your first stock? Why did you buy it, and what happened to it?

As an example, I will answer these questions from my personal experience. The first share I ever bought was the Intershop share. I bought it on July 16, 1998, when I was 17 years old. On that day, the share was launched on the stock exchange.

One day before that, it was possible to subscribe (order) the share for about 51 EUR. However, only a few people were lucky enough to get them. The share price started its first trading day at about 150 EUR. Since I did not get an allotment at 51 EUR, I had to buy it on the stock exchange at a higher price. If I remember correctly, I paid around 147 EUR. Then nothing happened in the months after that. At one point, the price dropped to 100 EUR, give or take. In the meantime, I turned 18 and needed money for my own car. At some point I sold my shares, probably for around 130 EUR. On March 13, 2000, about one year later, the share stood at just under 4,500 EUR! One year later, it was worth 250 EUR and in 2004, it was worth 15 EUR. At some point, the share was no longer even worth a single euro. Since a new currency, the euro, was introduced in Europe on January 1, 2001, some of the values that I mentioned above were converted from D-Mark, the former currency in Germany, to EUR.

Am I upset that I sold the stock too early? No, even today, I still experience situations like that on a regular basis. For this, it does not need a booming stock market like the one at the turn of the millennium. Lots of people bought the shares for 2,500 EUR, often financing the deal with a loan. Suddenly, the share price dropped by 30%. They kept the stock, hoping it would recover, and ended up losing 99% of their investments. Stock market psychology regularly ensures that cases like that (sitting out losses until a total loss is made) occur frequently. To be honest, I would have sold the Intershop shares at the latest at a 100% gain and would not have waited for further profits. In general, this is better than selling at a loss. There is a wisdom about the stock market: 'It is better to be sad about a missed profit than to be stuck in an investment that has just gone down the drain.'

When I was 18, I dreamed of moving to Frankfurt/Main, the financial centre in Germany, to become a stockbroker. Sitting on the pulse of the financial markets, bringing together crazy investors by shouting on the floor. But later, trading on the floor was almost non-existent. Computers had won. During my studies, I first wanted to become a fund manager and then an investment banker. I started my career at an investment bank in Frankfurt, where I learned a lot about the products sold to private and institutional investors. After some time, I moved to the portfolio management department of a fund company. I did not have to make investment decisions directly, but I had to evaluate them. In this function, I dealt with several hundred fund managers, implementing their investment decisions in the market, i.e., buying and selling bonds, shares, and foreign exchange buying and selling, sometimes for 100 million EUR. I shared their passion and often suffered with them. Along the way, I participated in various training courses, such as analyst training (CIIA) or the trader's licence of the derivatives exchange EUREX.

In my private life, I am often asked about stock exchange topics. Most people would like to know how to become millionaires. Looking back, I must have explained the financial markets so many times to different people that I could write a book. Well, this is exactly what I have done.

I would like to make you fit for the financial market and do not expect any basic knowledge from the reader. The goal is to show you how much you need to invest and at what age you need to invest in order to have the chance of a prosperous pension - without trembling and gambling. I have not used any other literature as sources for my book. Instead, I read what hardly anyone else reads or understands: the fine print in sales brochures. I wrote the book from a European perspective, with a special focus on Germany, so my examples are also in euro. Within the European Union, there are uniform rules for trade and regulation. In the event of significant deviations from European standards, I will point this out. You do not have to read every chapter of this book, but I recommend it, even if you have never planned to invest in bonds or commodities and just want to buy a few funds. From my experience, I can say that everything in the financial markets is interrelated. Therefore, it is mandatory to understand the basics of the stock market to successfully build up wealth.

Is it even possible to understand the stock market?

'The stock market - I don't understand it, it's too complicated for me.'

'The stock market is only for professionals or gamblers.'
'How does a share price evolve?'

Are you one of those who says these or similar sentences, think or has heard them from others? Do you need a degree, experience, a stock market license, or an adult education course to understand the stock market?

First of all, there is nobody who fully understands the stock market; there are certainly many people who know a lot. But because not everything is known and explainable, financial markets continue to offer much material for academic papers. If you meet someone who claims to fully understand the stock market, ask them how much they know. Ask what a risk-free interest rate is. Even if you get an answer or even a number, it will merely be based on their own opinion or a personal assessment of that person. By no means will the answer be a provable fact.

Studies: I studied economics because I took great interest in financial markets, first as a hobby and later as a profession. Microeconomics, price theory, game theory, and a fair share of business administration makes a good mixture for approaching the financial markets scientifically. But how the stock market really works, I did not learn at university. Most students of business administration or economics know little about the stock market at the end of their studies. Those with some solid knowledge joined a student association where they engaged in the stock exchange and looked for like-minded people.

Literature, stock market guides, and seminars: these deal directly with the subject of the stock market. You learn about individual aspects or products, and, assuming that you are really interested in the subject, you can take away some basic knowledge.

Literature: With this, you can acquire more than basic knowledge, but it is difficult to find the right level compared to your own knowledge. My book is aimed at newcomers, so it is kept simple and therefore easy to digest. But already at this level, it is difficult to see whether one's own level of knowledge is advanced enough not to be considered a beginner and to be ready to play with the big guys.

Experience: During an interview, when talking to applicants, trainees, or apprentices at the fund company for the first time, I do not care much about their previous training. Rather, I want to know if the person I am talking to has experience in the financial market (I am deliberately not just talking about stocks). I also would like to know whether there is at least one investment idea, if 1,000, 10,000, or 100,000 EUR are available. Why do I do this? This way I can find out how much the candidate is burning for the financial market. Is the applicant really interested in the topic or, even better, actively participating (this can also be done without any financial risk, e.g., stock exchange games)? Will their minds be stimulated in stock market seminars or when reading even the driest literature about the stock market?

With this book, I will introduce the most important products on the financial market as well as the relevant terminology. My explanations will help you immediately understand stock-related content from other sources (e.g., internet banking) or channels like YouTube and Wikipedia. In addition, you can use this knowledge to develop your own roadmap for your personal asset accumulation and see the big picture.

Basic knowledge: Securities Accounts and Investment Funds

Securities account

Before entering the world of investments, you need to have a securities account. Could you do without one? Well, in case you decide to invest in gold bars only, all you need is a vault. If you put your money in a savings account or a call money account, that is, if you invest in cash, you don't need to have a securities account either. If you own an annuity or endowment policy, which earns a return on capital on the financial markets for your future payouts, you can invest and speculate on the stock market without having a securities account. However, actively investing your money requires a securities account.

You did not know that you were already active in the stock market? Or that you are playing the stock market? Or even worse, you are investing in food and thus driving up prices, causing people in other parts of the world to starve? This book will show you what you need to know to do better in the future.

An 80-year-old man once told me that he did not have a remote understanding of my profession, had no idea about the stock market, and said that he would never invest in stocks. I had to explain to him that he was already playing the market much more intensively than I was.

Every day, when driving past the small gas station in town, he looked at the prices and monitored the ups and downs of the gas price. When he felt that the price had reached its lowest point, he would fill up the tank even though it was still half full. The next day, the man often saw that the gas price had dropped even further. Without realising it, he was speculating in oil, a commodity whose price is determined on the stock exchange.

For probably 50 years, he had played the lottery every week. Assuming a stake of 10 EUR per week, he spent 26,000 EUR over this long period of time. If he had invested conservatively 20,000 EUR in shares at the age of 30, he could have sold them for 1,000,000 EUR on his 80th birthday! Conservatively, mind you, no gambling stocks. He would have had to invest only 2,000 EUR in gambler shares, and the chance would have been perhaps 1:10 that they would also become worth 1 million. Whether 1:10 is the correct likelihood or perhaps 1:5 or even 1:30 would be more scientifically correct here, I do not know. However, playing the lottery with a chance of 1 in 140 million will certainly put it into perspective, and that is what I wanted to express to you.

I also realised that he had investment funds, which his bank advisors had talked him into. I only found out about it because he didn't understand his custody account statements and wanted me to tell him how much money was invested there. It was a full stock fund. The bank had set it up for him when he was already retired. At that time, there was a 4% interest rate on the call money. I will not comment further on that at this point. I will leave it to you to think about it again after you have read my book to the end.

I have met many people over the years who were not aware that they had a depot. They were between 20 and 80 years old. If you consciously want to set up a securities account, any bank will help you very quickly. It can be a branch bank, their online platform, or a direct bank (which are very popular, especially in Germany, Austria, and Switzerland). You will have to fill out some forms at the beginning, where they will ask you about your experience in the financial markets and your approximate financial circumstances. The banks do this not out of curiosity but because they are required to do so. They obviously may not allow you to make high-risk investments if you are a beginner and the investments do not exceed your financial possibilities. If the bank does not do this, they may be liable for possible financial losses. This is regulated by the EU (MiFiD). You will also be required to provide a clearing account.

Clearing account

A bank account, the so-called clearing account, is required for each securities account. This can be an account set up separately for securities transactions, a call money account, or your current account.

This is required to withdraw money for securities purchases or fees. When your securities pay out money or you sell them, the amounts go into this clearing account. As long as it doesn't incur additional charges, I recommend that you don't link the clearing account to your regular checking account. On the one hand, it can become very confusing if account movements on your checking account are permanently triggered by the securities account, and on the other hand, with deposits to the clearing account, you can control exactly what you want to invest and what not to invest.

For example, you want to buy security XYZ for 2,000 EUR. By mistake, you mistyped and did not pay attention to the number of units or price, and you accidentally placed a purchase order for 20,000 EUR. Believe me, this often happens even to professionals (enter 'fat finger' in the search engine). If you now use your current account as a settlement account and this is also sufficiently covered (e.g., due to an established overdraft facility on your current account), the purchase is carried out at 20,000 EUR.

Fees

When it comes to fees, there are securities-independent fees and charges that can be incurred when buying or selling.

When you place a buy or sell order in a securities account - this is called an **order** - in most cases, it will involve a fee, the **order fee or commission**. If a particular security costs nothing (this may be the case with some mutual funds), it's because the security itself includes annual fees that push down the price and benefit the bank. Nothing is for free!

Then, if the custody account has at least one security, there will be an annual custody fee in most cases. It can be compared to an account fee for the checking account. And as with the account fee for the current account, there are providers who take no fees at all and some who really charge. I will revisit the topic of choosing a custody account provider at the end of the book. I can give you advice on this only when you know for yourself what you want to invest in and whether you want to talk to an advisor about it again or whether you want to manage your securities account purely digitally.

The difference between branch bank and direct bank

When was the last time you went to a bank to speak to a bank advisor? The last time I left the house to do exactly that was about seven years ago. I used to have an 'old' account that was opened 25 years ago, and I had to change the type of that account. In the meantime, internet and cell phones have become so common that today even 70-year-olds do their banking online.

When it comes to stock exchange transactions, any branch bank will gladly open its doors and offer advice. Loans are not the way to make money in times of low interest rates. When the savings book still got you a 3% interest rate, banks took the savings book money from their customers to lend it for 6 or 8% to other customers that needed money. In 2021, you got a loan from as little as 2% in Europe. This is because European banks had to pay interest on deposits (current account balances of their customers, overnight deposits) to the Central Bank, in other words, negative interest rates. The banks have no interest in accepting money from you as a deposit and would rather grant loans at favourable but not very lucrative conditions to their customers. If someone exceeds the granted overdraft limit by taking out an insurance policy or buying securities (so-called commission business), which may even come from the bank itself, then the bank generates a nice margin. This applies to both branch and direct banks.

However, the branch bank will always add the advisory service for purchasing securities to the bill. Regardless of whether you asked for an opinion or if the given advice was good or bad. Advising also means giving recommendations or an analysis of individual shares. These are passed on to the advisors so that they can answer questions from their customers, such as 'What do you think of share XYZ?' easily and quickly. Recommendations usually reflect the bank's opinion and are not the result of your advisor's own analysis. Each and every customer of a bank will get the same information.

Direct banks work differently. The customer will not receive advice from a direct bank, which makes their service significantly cheaper. However, this does not stop them from sending out advertisements for financial products. Detailed analysis of individual stocks is not as common. Market reports or risk analyses on the securities account are available depending on the provider. Within the last 20 years, direct banks have dominated the market when it comes to security trading; however, they can also be found in Austria and Switzerland.

The securities identification number

Whenever you own something that is labelled with a securities identification number, you need to have a securities account.

The German Securities Identification Number (so-called WKN) consists of six digits and can contain numbers or letters. Each WKN comes with its own International Identification Number, the ISIN. The ISIN consists of twelve digits and often begins with a country code (e.g., DE, FR, LU). Sometimes it starts with a code that indicates the technical processing (e.g., XS). In the US and Canada only the ISIN is used.

The identification numbers are available for everything that you cannot directly hold in your hands but that can still be owned, even if it exists somewhere on a sheet of paper. The proof that the paper belongs to you is your securities account. It is basically a list that contains the identification numbers of your shares or papers, how many you own, and what they are currently worth. By the way, you can enter the identification numbers into an internet search engine, and it will take you to the financial information sites where you can see the current price.

Investment funds - when others do the work for you

Why should you do all the work and deal with stocks, bonds, and the like, when you can put your money in investment funds which are managed by professionals?

A private investor can hardly judge whether the professional, i.e., the fund manager, is good or not. The private investor sees the result, and that, admittedly, is the most important thing. Beyond that, he may have one or two other fund ratios at his disposal, which provide information about operating costs or risks. Independently, whether the manager is good or not, the fund is going to come at a cost. Usually at the time of acquisition during the guaranteed holding period and often when the fund is sold. There are funds where the manager actively decides what to buy (so-called target funds) and funds where the manager attempts to emulate an index (ETFs). In both cases, the fund is a special secured asset and indices play a role in both. As secured assets, the investments are protected from the insolvency of the issuing company (e.g., Blackrock, Amundi, DWS). Therefore, I will explain these separately.

The investment fund

In Germany, funds (collective investment schemes) are set up by a **financial investment management company**, which administers the assets. Administration includes, among other things, accounting, fund price calculation, risk management, the preparation of all legal documents, legal reporting, and the monitoring of investment limits.

A fund manager does not necessarily have to be part of the capital management company. There are companies that are run by only two or three fund managers who make investment decisions. They communicate their investment ideas to the responsible capital management company, which then checks the feasibility and finally instructs the trading company to place an order. Both trading and sales can take place outside of the financial investment management company. The assets are held in custody by the custodian, which can be somehow compared to a securities account. The depositary is always a credit institution. When you buy a fund, the depositary will give you shares by transferring them to your private custody account.

Within the EU, investment funds are regulated and are called UCITS (Undertakings for Collective Investment in Transferable Securities). Simply put, they are funds in which the legislator protects retail investors by setting important rules such as risk diversification, prohibition of highly speculative transactions, and publication obligations (prospectus, reports). An investment fund is considered a special form of asset of the capital management company and the depositary, and it is not mixed with the company's other assets or even other funds. Its most important characteristic is that it is protected from the insolvency of the company or depositary.

Accumulating or distributing of dividends

Funds, both target funds and ETFs, can be distributed or accumulated. A fund that distributes pays income into your clearing account. This method guarantees that no one can take your earnings away from you. But the distributed money does not earn any more money until you invest it again somewhere. The accumulating fund automatically reinvests all earnings, which leads to compound interest and promises better returns in the long term.

I will spare you the exact tax implications and technology. You will pay taxes with both options. With the distributing fund, you pay more during the holding period; with the one that accrues dividends, you get more when you sell it. In total, the tax burden is the same as for income. It is important to set up an exemption order for capital gains with your bank, as the tax is only due once the mentioned amount has been exceeded. Without that exemption order, the first euro of profit is taxed. The taxes are usually paid directly by your bank to the tax and revenue office.

Indices

If you are thinking about investing in funds, you should look at indices. An index is a compilation of investments (index members) bound to defined rules and with a certain theme. At the time of the index's launch, it starts at a certain level, for example, 100 or 1,000 points. Depending on how the index members perform and what the rules say, subsequently, the points change up or down.

This sounds a lot like a fund. In fact, there are many similarities, but the price movements of the index members and the set of rules alone determine their weighting. No human being intervenes by buying or selling securities.

Indices now exist for almost everything that can be quantified with a monetary value. Quantifying with monetary value means that there is a neutral price determination. This is the case with exchange-traded products.

From a German perspective, the DAX® and Dow Jones are certainly the most famous, as they regularly appear in the German news, especially when their prices fall sharply.

Since indices, in the case of stocks, give a good overview of which countries or which industries are currently rising or falling, they are often simply referred to as the 'market.' The market is strong or rising. The market is falling or is weak. The market is going crazy, or it fluctuates. As a rule, this always refers to the development of the most important indices.

What does this have to do with mutual funds? A successful fund manager beats the market. In other words, his fund outperformed an index that emulates roughly the same theme.

So, indices are a level of comparison here, also called **benchmarks**.

Target funds

The launch

The target fund is a classic among investment funds. A fund manager has an idea with which he can strategically increase or protect people's money from loss, wants to be rewarded, and is remunerated with a management fee. He establishes a fund; this fund is given a securities identification number, and anyone who has a securities account can buy shares in the fund. Since a fund has fixed costs from the very first day of its existence (for example, auditors or publication costs), it can only start with a book value of EUR 5 million. Otherwise, the fixed costs would have a negative impact on the fund's results, which the investors pay indirectly.

To ensure that a target fund has an appropriate size at the start, a fund manager will look for an institutional investor. At the beginning, this investor will provide the fund with seed money. This can usually be any amount between EUR 10 million and EUR 50 million. However, the institutional investor will not pay the usual management fee of perhaps 1% per year, but only a fraction of it, or perhaps even nothing at all. In order to be able to calculate different fees for different types of investors, it is necessary that a target fund be launched with at least two tranches (and thus two security identification numbers): the expensive tranche for the retail investors and the cheaper one for the institutional investors. A tranche is like a class on a plane. The same performance or speed, but different prices.

Does that sound unfair to you? Well, it isn't. Institutional investors did not win the lottery but rather managed money from private individuals who already paid them a fee. Investors can be, for example, pension funds or insurance companies, which are remunerated through parts of their members' premiums.

The initial charge

When purchasing shares of a target fund, you will most likely pay an initial charge, which can easily be as much as 5% of the market value of the shares you want to buy. So, you pay a 5% premium, and your investment is immediately negative. Now you must trust that the fund soon achieves a particularly good result in order to recoup the paid commission.

The initial charge goes to the sales department as a commission even if you have chosen the fund yourself and no advisory service was given. Sometimes, banks promote funds for a short period of time without or with only half the usual premium. This can especially happen if the sales department and management are from the same company. If the fund is struggling with draining cash (many investors are selling their shares), it is quite conceivable that the sales department will offer an incentive to buy shares to soften the impact of the diminishing cash.

Tip: When you have selected a fund and its fund volume is large (over EUR 100 million), you can also buy shares via a fund exchange. Instead of 5%, you are only charged 1% to 2%, including order fees. If you have an online custody account and enter the order there, do not select KVG (i.e., the fund company) as the exchange (i.e., the fund company), but an exchange (if available). If you manage your securities account through a branch bank with an advisor, the advisor will do everything to convince you to trade through the KVG; otherwise, he will earn almost nothing. The best thing to do is to enter on the various financial websites on the Internet the securities identification number (e.g., onvista.de, finanzen.net, boerse.de) and then click on Trading venues. There you can see whether there are other exchanges besides the KVG that trade the fund, and you are therefore better prepared to argue with your bank advisor.

The hard life of the fund manager - the hunt for alpha

What does a fund manager actually do?

When I was still a student and visited a bond fund manager with my investment club from university, I was told: 'You can get a 3% risk-free interest on the market at the moment. All day I would be looking for ways on how to get 3.5% without any risk.' I was trying to beat the market—in that case, the interest rate market.

Two years after the visit, the bond fund manager's employer no longer existed. The reason behind that is the bad mortgage loans (ABS/MBS) that the company acquired from the US. These had promised 4% risk-free interest but were in fact risky (subprime) and went down the drain in 2007.

Equity fund managers also try to beat the market. The market is usually an index that is comparable to the respective fund profile. A 'global equities' manager will not have the DAX® as his benchmark but rather the MSCI World, which represents the largest companies in the world. If the shares of the benchmark rise, so too will the fund since it holds similar stocks as the index. Easy as pie.

However, being better than the market is an art. Be it that the fund rises more in market phases or that it does not fall as much when the market goes down, this positive difference to the market is called 'Alpha' or 'outperforming the market.' Fund managers are constantly looking for strategies to generate Alpha. When they fail to do so, investors will wonder why they are paying a management fee. If they would have invested directly in the market, see ETF, no fee would have been due, and as a result, the performance would have been better.

Being a fund manager is not an easy job. When they are not looking for Alpha, they have to justify their performance (especially to institutional investors) or raise new money.

The fund price calculation

The price of a fund is calculated independently by the capital management company and the depositary. Both entities should come up with the same result. If this is not the case, a reconciliation must take place between the two. If both parties agree, the fund price is published.

Basically, fund price calculation follows this pattern:

In a first step, the value of the fund assets is calculated.

   Value of all assets
+ pending gains and losses
+ receivables and liabilities
= fund assets (technical term NAV - Net Asset Value)

Dividing the value of the fund assets by the number of fund units in circulation results in the fund price.

Every fund price has a trading date and a settlement date. The trading date is the valuation date, and the prices (noon or closing prices) of the respective day are used for valuation. Since the close of the market must be awaited, the management company and the depositary can only determine the fund's price retrospectively and can only calculate the price the following day. One day later, the settlement date takes place. On this day, purchases and sales of fund units are settled by the investors.

Example: Today is notionally February 1. Up until a certain time (the so called 'cut off,' usually in the afternoon), investors may place buy or sell orders for fund shares. On February 2, the capital management company and custodians will determine the fund price for February 1 (the trading day), which will be calculated and published. On February 3, the buy or sell orders from February 1 will be settled on the account at the price of February 1.

This example is the standard, but there are funds that differ from it. However, on a bad market day (which will cause the price of the fund to fall), it will never be possible to just sell the shares at the good price of the previous day.

Risks

Performance
Is it possible that a mutual fund suffers a total loss? In theory, that is possible, however, this will hardly happen as funds are required by law to spread their risk and to also comply with certain risk parameters. Nonetheless, there are cases where

funds lose 70% of their unit value. Usually, low-performing funds will be terminated by the capital management company due to a lack of buyers and the fact that many investors will sell shares, making the fund smaller. With the outflows and poor performance, the fund will eventually be too small to cover its fixed costs in an economically reasonable way.

Liquidity

Funds that partly invest in assets that are difficult to sell come with some risk. It might take some time before you will be able to sell your shares and get paid out; this can be worse than a poorly performing fund. As a rule, only the return of the money is delayed until the fund has managed to sell the illiquid assets.

Black box

Unfortunately, as a private investor, you do not see what your fund manager is doing; he acts in a black box. Let's assume you were able to peek into that black box. There is Fund Manager A: Who, maybe once a week, checks the investments and just plays golf the rest of the week.

Then there is Fund Manager B: He checks the financial markets every day, reacting immediately when something happens, even while on vacation (or from the golf course).

Who would you trust with your hard-earned money? Probably B.

Who would I give my money to? A!

Why is that? Fund manager A acts like an index. He has his strategy, does not tinker with it permanently, and in the end is usually more successful.

Sometimes, it does happen that a type A manager becomes a type B. Especially when things are going badly. Then the number of trades in the fund increases, and the performance usually gets worse. Unfortunately, you don't get to see it; that's the 'black box' risk.

Practical tip

If you decide to buy a target-date fund, I've created the following checklist for your selection:

1. Try to understand the strategy and risk of the fund. Read the mandatory documents and descriptions.

2. Choose a fund that has been in existence for several years and has gone through good and bad market phases. How did the fund develop in the crisis years of 2008 (subprime), 2011 (Fukushima), or 2020 (Corona)? The market has recovered from all these crises and recovered all losses; what about the fund?

3. Take a fund with a volume of at least EUR 100 million. In general, as a rule, several institutional investors will have chosen the fund, too. And they are your best advocate.

4. Try to avoid the issue surcharges by buying the shares on a fund exchange.

5. Be suspicious if the fund is offered through advertising; a well-performing fund does not need any advertising.

6. Find your funds at financial websites in the 'Funds' section and use the filter according to your interests.

7. Don't forget to set up an exemption order. If you still have a savings account or a call money account, reduce the balance there to a minimum (especially in times of low interest rates) and rather increase the amount in your securities account.

These are basic tips. Most relevant to your investment success is the theme (stocks, bonds, commodities, currency). Before we can discuss themes, the different investment objects need to be explained. Once this is done, I will come back to this topic.

ETF

Can we buy just the market?

Exchange-Traded Funds (ETF) point from their name to an essential characteristic regarding the purchase. It is traded on a stock exchange, like a share. This has two advantages: First, there is no issue surcharge, and second, you can follow the fund price every second.

The term 'index fund' is however much more appropriate and is now used as a synonym for ETFs. Each index tracks one market: Germany, USA, Europe, Asia, developing countries, the world, large stocks, small stocks, technology, healthcare, banking & finance, automotive, sustainable stocks, high dividend stocks, commodities with agriculture, commodities without agriculture, bonds – there is an index for everything that can be calculated. If there is an index, there is now almost always an ETF that mirrors it exactly.

For most target funds, there is an index that can be used as a comparison. Historically, it has been observed that in the long run, in most cases (but often also in the short run), the index has performed better. A rational investor, i.e., someone who leaves emotion out of the equation when making investment decisions when looking at statistics, prefers to opt for the ETF right away. So, he buys the market. If now a target fund will not beat the market, he will achieve a better result.

The indices

The market for ETFs is booming. While in the beginning ETFs were indices, today new indices are invented every day in order to be able to launch an ETF on them. There are companies for which index creation and management is the most important business models. The famous Dow Jones from the media is actually called the Dow Jones Industrial Average. Dow Jones is the name of the company that calculates it. The STOXX company calculates around 300 indices, of which the most famous is the 'EuroStoxx 50.'

Have you ever heard of the index: 'Scientific Beta Japan HFI Multi-Beta Multi-Strategy Six Factor EW Market Beta Adjusted (Leverage)'? It really exists, and of course there is also an ETF on it. I need to do some research on this, as I don't know much about it or what it does. Scientific Beta is the index provider, and Japanese stocks are not selected by size but by six factors. If you cannot find easy-to-read information about an index with an ETF on it on the Internet, you're buying a pig in a poke. I would not do it.

The costs

If a fund company wants to replicate an index in a fund, there are three options:

a) Buying all index members according to their weighting (physical replication). However, since the weightings in the index change daily due to market movements, the index members in the fund must also be constantly adjusted. Making adjustments always costs money—the so-called transaction costs. This is reflected in the fund costs accordingly.

b) Investing only in the index heavyweights and leaving out the insignificant members. Required adjustments are less but will still result in the approximate index performance. The fund costs therefore become more favourable.

c) Replicate the index synthetically, i.e., artificially. To do this, financial contracts such as swaps or futures, which I will discuss later, will be used. This is the cheapest option.

Regardless of which option the company chooses, it beats the price of the traditional target funds by far. The ETF does not need a fund manager; it only needs a computer. The better the computer is, the lower the running costs are.

Risks

Market risk

If the market falls, the ETF is fully exposed and cannot defend itself, therefore reducing its investment quota. Worse: When the markets fall, the ETF must also sell, and as a result, the market falls even further. As long as the markets recover and eventually reach an all-time high, the ETF will also recover, unless you bet on the wrong theme.

Theme risk

There are indexes that have not recovered as quickly in the past, for example the ATHEX Composite (a Greek benchmark index). After being at around 1,500 points in 2004 and at the end of 2007 at over 5,000 points, it fell well below 1,000 points during the course of the debt crisis. Ten years later, it was still there. If you bet on sector indices, it becomes particularly dangerous. The EuroStoxx Banks (yes, banks) have lost 80% in only two years. With a result like that, any target fund manager would have quit. So, it is important to choose a broadly diversified index or to diversify yourself by buying several ETFs, each of which tracks a different sector.

Practical tips

I also have a few tips for ETFs.

1. Only buy ETFs if you know what the index behind it is doing.

2. For large indices, there are usually several ETF providers (Ishares, Xtracker, Amundi, etc.). All of

them work the same way. So, there is no need to worry about different performances when choosing. ETFs are safe from the insolvency of the provider. However, the costs may vary among the different providers.

3. If there are several providers for one index that use the same replication method, compare the costs.

4. Look for your funds at financial websites in the section 'ETF' and filter according to your interests.

As with the target funds, I will describe the theme selection later in this book.

What role your bank or insurance broker plays

There are many fund management companies in the world, quite a few manage more than EUR 100 billion in fund assets (spread over thousands of funds). Do you know Blackrock or Pimco? These are the largest fund companies in the world, but they mainly manage the money of institutional investors. Therefore, they are often unknown to the private investor. Although in the case of Blackrock, the sub-brand 'Ishares' as an ETF provider is familiar to some.

On the other hand, in Germany, DEKA, Union Investment, or DWS will likely ring a bell if you are a customer of a savings bank, a Volksbank, or the Deutsche Bank, because they are their house fund companies. When DEKA launches a mutual fund in Germany, the savings banks are asked to collect money from their customers. This is basically the same all over the world. Every bank has its own distribution channels.

Is that reprehensible? Not necessarily because all fund managers, regardless of the company, are fishing in the same pond. There are good and bad managers in every company. If you buy funds and ETFs from your bank's own provider, you may have a price advantage over the funds from other companies because they are offered to you at a lower price as a group customer. Feel free to look at the offers, but be cautious if the bank advisor recommends something.

Insurance brokers do not always act independently, either. The fact that a broker working for Allianz offers funds from Allianz Global Investors (AGI) to his clients should not come as a surprise. But the fact that DVAG is a sales partner of DWS funds is not obvious at first glance. If your broker can give you qualified reasons why fund XYZ is good, there is nothing to stop you from buying an in-house fund. But what is a qualified justification?

Not qualified:

'Fund XYZ has performed great in the past.'

Note from me: The past says nothing about the future. This is also stated in the investor documentation that you will be given.

'Fund XYZ will perform great in the future.'

Note from me: This statement will not come so directly, because the advisor would make himself liable. However, he may be able to subtly convey it. Example: 'The theme of the fund is, after all, a booming market at the moment' or 'The fund is market-neutral; it can make profits no matter in which direction the market goes.'

'For fund XYZ, we have a special offer right now. The acquisition fees are cut in half or waived for a short time.'

Note from me: You don't get anything out of this if the fund is performing poorly or has expensive management fees. If you have neutrally selected a fund that is still currently on offer, then congratulations! Go for it!

Qualified:

'Fund XYZ has the best cost structure among comparable funds of the same investment theme.'

'With fund XYZ, you spread your risk across the overall portfolio.'

'With Fund XYZ, you are betting on the broad industry, except tobacco and gambling, just as you wanted.'

The bank advisor may have a default on what he should sell, so he is not an independent advisor. If he recommends, on his own initiative and without you having asked him, low-commission products (e.g., ETFs), he is one of the better advisors. To help you understand the important-sounding fund names and the strategies in fund prospectuses, in the next chapter I will explain the terms used in the fund world as well as the most important terms from the financial world.

Terms from the fund world

Long/Short - or simply the side

No matter what is traded in the financial market, whether it is stocks, bonds, commodities, foreign exchange - there will always be investors who are convinced that a market is going up and those who see it differently. Maybe they even want to bet on that.

Let's leave speculators aside for a moment. A commodity supplier will get into trouble if his commodity falls in price. He will no longer be able to sell it at a price that covers the costs. On the financial market, it is possible to hedge against this. He can buy products that give him a payout if his raw material falls. Of course, this comes at a cost because it is an insurance policy. The more likely it is that the commodity will drop dramatically (for example, due to historical fluctuations), the more expensive the premium becomes.

If someone holds shares directly or indirectly through funds, he will probably sell them at some point. Maybe the investment goal has been reached, the money is needed, or the feeling is going around that a big crash is coming.

Whether through speculators, hedgers, or profit-takers, there is a market for buying and selling on both sides. Therefore, the positioning in the buy or sell direction is also called a 'side.' If there were no two sides, trading could not be done in the first place, and there wouldn't be a functioning market.

A market participant who is betting on rising prices is long. On the other hand, a participant who bets on falling prices is short. It may be technical jargon, but if you buy an ETF called 'Short DAX®,' it must be clear to you that the fund will only make a profit if the DAX® falls.

Beware, trap! When it comes to bond funds, 'long' does not mean that you are betting on rising interest rates. If the fund is called 'Short Duration,' it doesn't even have anything to do with the side. In the case of foreign exchange, you must also think carefully about whether you will make any profits with 'long EUR' if the EUR/USD rate rises from 1.20 to 1.30 or falls from 1.20 to 1.10.

I will come to bonds and currencies later. It is very important to understand that long and short refer to the buy or sell side, but can have various meanings in different markets. There may also be alternative terms for long and short. A long-lasting sustained rise in the market has its own symbol: the bull. Anyone who bets on rising markets is correspondingly bullish. The opposite, the long falling market, is symbolised by a bear. If you bet on falling markets, you are bearish. An ETF name that contains the word 'bull' is long (bull market). If it comes with a 'bear' it is short (bearish market).

Value /Growth – Stock picking

Looking at equity fund management, value and growth are the two predominant strategies in stock picking. The aim is to select stocks from a given theme or field that will outperform other stocks in the same field in the future. It is not always possible to draw a clear line; it may be that a stock is equally interesting to a value manager as it is to a colleague who follows the growth style.

Value

The value investor invests in companies that are already established in the market with a business model that continues to be promising and with a stock market value that appears to be too low. The investor uses valuation techniques, compares the companies with their competitors and tries to analyse the success of the business model in the future. If he adds up all the analyses and comes to the result that company XYZ is worth EUR 2 billion but has a value of only EUR 1.5 billion on the stock market, he buys the share.

Whether this approach is promising?

On the one hand:

- In times of crisis, the overall market falls, even though not all shares are affected by the crisis. This can even be amplified by ETFs on the market because they reduce all their values when the overall market is falling. Amazon stocks fell at the beginning of the Corona pandemic or Electric utilities in the financial market crisis. These stocks recovered the fastest, because even newcomers to the market without great analyst skills could recognise that these were value stocks.
- Since value stocks are usually good dividend payers, it is often worthwhile buying even if the bet (the stock that is undervalued at the moment) does not work out.

On the other hand:

As long as no one possesses insider information (information that the public does not have) and exploits it (this is punishable by law), the share price reflects all available information about a company. The exceptions are times of crashes, where all rules are often suspended. But precisely then no one dares to buy. There is a stock market saying: 'Never reach for a falling knife,' and many value investors adhere to this.

Warren Buffet is one of the most famous and successful value investors. He is not necessarily known for analysing stocks and strikes when he thinks they are too cheap. However, he evaluates the success of the business model and holds his investments for a very long time. There may also be a misstep, but this is made up for many times over by successful decisions.

Growth

When companies are not yet making a profit or if they are making only little profit but have strong potential for the future, they are also called growth stocks. The term growth expresses a common investment strategy. Investors are not interested in what has been achieved so far. They are rather interested in the future performance of a company. The risk is higher with growth. If the forecast is right about the future market, it is not yet clear whether the selected company will be able to capitalise on it. A company that has not made profits in the past has not yet shown that it can do so in the future.

Can this approach be successful?

There is a case for it:

> If we assume that all the information about a company is known, the current value of the company should be fairly valued on the stock market. The growth investor is not bothered by this even if the company is perhaps too expensive. In any case, he is betting on the future which nobody can predict.
> With this strategy there can also be a misjudgment from time to time, without jeopardising the overall result of all investments. Growth stocks are candidates for doubling or triple their value within a reasonable period of time. This potential often makes up for individual losses.

Arguing against:

> Which industry will be successful in the future and
> which company can take advantage of it is a very
> difficult assessment to make. Here, the fund manager
> must not only be an expert in the sector, but also an
> expert in economics. Many are the latter. But when it
> comes to the knowledge of the sector, especially of the
> ones that only emerged recently, things can get tricky.
> In a mutual fund, the strategy is difficult to implement.
> It must diversify the shares, most of which may only
> account for a 5% share. Besides that, only four of them
> may have a maximum weighting of 10% in the fund.
> So if there are one or two price rockets in the mix, they
> quickly exceed the 10% share and must be sold again
> and again, until they fall below this threshold. This
> profit-taking also has advantages, but it makes it more
> difficult for the strong stocks to make up for the losses
> of the weaker ones.

In general, to summarise Value and Growth strategies, it can
be said: The legal restrictions on investment funds, but also
performance pressure, can cause difficulties even for an
experienced fund manager.

Balanced fund

A fund that invests in bonds and equities is a mixed fund and
often has the term 'balanced' in the fund name. To find out
whether a fund invests in bonds or equities in a balanced way
or sees bonds as an admixture to an equity fund, this
information must unfortunately be looked up in the sales
documents. If you want to set up your securities portfolio with

exactly 50% bonds and 50% stocks, you should probably choose one fund with stocks and one bond fund.

Hedge funds and hedge

Hedge Funds

Once when I did not know anything about hedge funds, someone explained it to me like this: 'A hedge fund makes a profit, no matter what.' Today, I would explain it a bit differently: 'A hedge fund tries to make a profit in all market phases and also uses unconventional techniques.'

Explaining what techniques are used and their assessment would easily fill an entire book. I will therefore only list what I consider to be the two most famous techniques, which are not used when managing a normal investment fund (UCITS).

> **Short Selling**: A hedge fund can borrow shares and sell them in order to buy them back later at a lower price (if they have dropped) and then return them back to the lender. The strategy does not require rising markets. If the bet does not pan out and the stock rises, the fund must buy back at whatever price. This can wipe out all the fund's assets.
>
> **Leverage:** A hedge fund can borrow and thus increase its exposure i.e., leverage it. A 100 million fund that takes a 40 million loan because it is sure to earn more than it has to pay in interest on the loan, is invested with a 140% exposure.

The word hedge fund is a term that is used daily in the institutional finance world, the same as in your garden, in the financial world a hedge offers protection.

A hedge fund is meant to be an alternative to conventional funds which regularly make losses in weak market phases. With a hedge fund the market phase should not matter. Mutual funds can also bet on falling prices even though they are not allowed to make short sales. For that there is the huge world of derivatives, which can be used to bet on financial market events whether someone is long or short. Long-term borrowing is prohibited for funds. As a maximum, they are allowed to borrow up to 10% of their assets in the short term. However, derivatives give them the opportunity to raise the stakes. By law, up to 200% of the usual market risk is possible. The evasion possibilities of the techniques tempt one or the other UCITS fund to present itself in its strategy as a hedge fund even when it is not allowed to call itself one. That is the reason why I mention it in this chapter. Just because the original purpose of the hedge fund was to secure the fund's assets, you cannot assume a risk-reducing product.

Hedge

For investors, the term 'hedge' itself is to be understood as a protection mechanism. Usually it is used to protect a fund (a hedge) against currency risks. If you buy shares of a fund that invests in dollar assets, you will have an indirect currency risk. A fund with 'EUR hedged' in its name hedges the currency risks. There are also derivatives for this purpose. The term is often found in ETFs or on certificates. An active fund manager usually hedges his currency risk anyway, because if he picks the right stocks, he will not let the currency influence the overall result.

But currency hedging comes at a cost. Especially if the currency to be hedged is not particularly stable. The annual fee will reduce the returns and, in extreme cases, can make an ETF as expensive as a target fund.

Total Return / Absolute Return

The very similar-sounding terms 'Total Return' and 'Absolute Return' are very popular in the active mutual fund world, and they have one thing in common: they try to get away from the classical benchmark thinking of the market. They promise gains independent of market performance, and their goal is often an annual return on market interest + X. An exact definition is difficult to give because each fund company defines it for itself. To find out details, it is often necessary to look deeper into the sales documents, if that is possible at all. Nevertheless, I will try to summarise the general understanding.

Absolute Return Funds

To make profits as much as possible, regardless of whether stocks or bonds rise or fall, is usually the goal of an 'Absolute Return.' A popular means of achieving this is the sale of risk premiums. The odds are such that the market will not rise or fall to threshold X within six months. For this, there is a premium. If the betting event does not occur, the fund can keep the premium. If the outcome occurs or becomes more likely to occur long before the cut-off date, the fund must enter the counter bet in order to hedge. The premium it then has to pay is many times higher, so it becomes very expensive. The strategy often works for years, but at some point, the market strikes unexpectedly and mercilessly.

Tip: If you want to buy a fund that does something with premiums or promises an absolute return, you should look at how long it has been in existence and how it has performed in times of crisis.

Total Return Funds

If a fund is flexible in its choice of investment classes, it can include equities, bonds, commodities, foreign exchange, or money market products. Theoretically, it could always invest in those things that are not in a downtrend. So it would always be possible, despite stock exchanges, to have a return, whether through price gains, dividends, or interest. A return from the 'total' universe of the financial market is possible. Hence the name 'Total Return.'

Unfortunately, the term is also used in other places in the financial world, where it can be encountered by private investors. Therefore, caution is advised, and not all that glitters is gold.

A total return index, for example, is an index that reinvests the theoretically distributed earnings of its members. This is the case with the DAX® Index. The price of the DAX® Index reflects the total return.

Sustainable / ESG / SRI

Green and sustainable are on everyone's lips and the absolute trend in the fund world. Older funds that invest only in sustainable companies, sometimes have the word 'sustainable' in their names. In the meantime, the labels ESG (Environmental Social Governance) and SRI (Socially Responsible Investment) are becoming established in the market. ESG is something specifically European.

The EU obliges investment funds to classify (disclosure regulation). This is done on the basis of the binding investment strategies with respect to ESG criteria, similar to the Nutri-Score on food packages. The most important criteria are environment, social, and good corporate governance.

The EU has defined in the Taxonomy Regulation what is actually meant by the three upper criteria defined by the EU in the Taxonomy Regulation. The criteria are developed on an ongoing basis. However, each fund or index can define differently how it takes ESG into account, as long as it stays within the bounds of what is legally possible.

Example: An index provider that calculates a stock index would like to release the stock index as an ESG variant. For this, he defines the E (Environmental) through the exclusion of companies that sell coal or nuclear power plants. S (Social) is fulfilled by excluding companies that sell coal or nuclear power plants that make their money from armaments or tobacco. For G (Governance), companies must allow work councils or disclose their compensation policy. The index provider throws out some energy suppliers (because of nuclear power), some airlines (because of armaments), or companies without works councils.

Thus, with little effort, an index was given the ESG seal. In practice, reference is often made to an ESG score, i.e., a score that attempts to measure sustainability. If a company with poor governance is far ahead on the environmental front, the other criteria pull it out of the bottom ranks and into the middle, making the company investable again.

What does this mean for you? Do not confuse the ESG label with a BIO seal. You are not necessarily investing in green stocks. Sustainability is so much in vogue that stock corporations are now 'bending' themselves over backwards to conform to ESG in order not to be seen as irresponsible corporations.

Counterparty / Issuer

The terms 'counterparty' and 'issuer' come up frequently in the financial world. Often, they are used as synonyms, but they can also describe different things.

Issuer

If someone in the market issues a security, he is an issuer. A company can issue shares or bonds. Investment banks issue certificates. Investment companies issue funds, although the more correct term here is 'launch.'

Counterparty

If the repayment of your invested money depends on the creditworthiness of a business partner, this business partner is called a counterparty. In this context, one speaks of counterparty risk for the person who lends the money.

Similarities and differences

In the case of bonds and certificates, you have a counterparty risk with the issuer. When it comes to stocks, you are a part owner of the issuer. The corporation is therefore not your counterparty. Nevertheless, you have a problem as a shareholder if the company in which you have invested is insolvent. Fund companies are not counterparties of yours; they manage your money, which is a special asset and therefore insolvency-proof. However, it may be that the fund that manages your money makes a deal with counterparties.

Asset classes - the investment objects

The term 'asset classes' is probably not familiar to most newcomers, so I will start from the beginning.

Assets: Everything that a fund manager or you in your private portfolio can buy, sell, or dispose of in your portfolio is an asset.

Why isn't it called a stock? Because there are many other assets that an investor can buy, many of which you will probably know. If you look at your checking account, you will see one asset: money, even if your account is in the negative. There are investors who take out loans in EUR and have the equivalent in USD, so the bottom line is not in the negative, just to somehow make money out of the constellation. Funds that you might want to buy would also be assets. There are a lot of professional fund managers who only buy funds and do not buy a single share; we are talking about so-called funds of funds.

Fund managers who decide which products go into their portfolio (the assets in the fund) are called asset managers. If someone only buys stocks, he is said to be only active in the asset class of equities. In fact, he will however always have some bank balances in his fund and is therefore active in at least two asset classes. With that, the term 'asset classes' should be clear now; in short, they are investment categories.

The distribution of investments among different asset classes is known as asset allocation.

On the next few pages, I will go into detail about each asset class. I will explain them and create the basic knowledge for investing in the different asset classes. This will help you understand the opportunities and risks on the one hand and, on the other hand, how they work.

Shares

The public limited company

If someone has a business idea and starts a company, he usually needs money. The money to start a business often comes from savings or perhaps from sponsors (or family). If the sponsor is not part of the family (as part of a gift or an inheritance), it is not uncommon to demand a share in the company or future profits, or at least the repayment of a loan that may have been given.

Entrepreneurs usually start as a personally liable legal entity (e.g., as a merchant) and are, with sufficient private securities or guarantees, welcomed by the banks as borrowers. If the company fails, creditors can access the private assets of the shareholder in order to satisfy their debts.

If the company and its risk grow due to external factors (which may also include employees), the type of business ownership of that company often will change to a corporation to limit the liability risk of the entrepreneur. Imagine, someone builds up a solid company, and due to a mistake by a single employee, it is destroyed. If, consequently, the private property of the entrepreneur is liable, it can get ugly. In addition to an economic crisis, external factors can also include regulation (e.g., tax legislation) or crime.

A limited liability company, the classic among corporations in Germany, can be set up quickly, but what appears to be advantageous at first glance also has its disadvantages. If a company does not make steady, secure, and timely profits, there will be no money available for company expansion. Who lends money to someone who is not yet making any or few profits if, in the event of the company's failure, they are not even fully liable?

Corporations can, given sufficient securities, take out loans. This is known as borrowed capital. In this case, capital is provided by a third party that has no influence on the borrower's business but is remunerated with interest. The counterpart to debt capital is equity capital. In that case the company acquires capital from someone who, in return, has a stake in the company. If the company is divided into a certain number of shares and each share is sold to investors in the form of a share certificate, the company becomes a corporation. The money paid for the shares goes directly to the company and allows investments and growth. The issuance of shares can be private to a select circle or publicly for anyone to invest.

The Initial Public Offering - Primary Market

When a share is offered for sale to the public for the first time, it is called an IPO (Initial Public Offering).

In simplified terms, it works like this: A company is estimated to be worth EUR 100 million. As part of an IPO, it offers 10 million shares at a price of 8 EUR to 12 EUR. Then anyone can submit offers with the number of shares (e.g., 10,000) and price (e.g., 9.5 EUR), the so-called subscription.

Why does the company not offer the shares for 10 EUR (10 x 10 million is 100 million after all)? because the EUR 100 million is an estimate.

If the estimate is incorrect and most investors estimate the company's value at EUR 85 million, no one or only a few will subscribe to the shares, and the IPO will be a failure without any significant return. If investors place bids for an average of 11EUR and all available shares are subscribed, the company will receive EUR 110 million. At this point, the stock exchange is not yet in play; here, the shares are sold directly by the company to the investors - this is called the primary market.

The stock market - the secondary market

Once the shares are distributed through the primary market, then comes the day of listing (when the shares are issued).

I am talking about stock exchanges in general; there are hundreds around the world and some in Germany. They are also called secondary markets. Not every share issued is listed on all stock exchanges. Each stock exchange has its own requirements for listing (e.g., on sales prospectuses, publication requirements, etc.). For a share to be accessible to the public, it must be listed on at least one stock exchange. The stock exchange provides the price quotation (the stock exchange price) during its opening hours.

The stock exchange price

How does the price on the stock exchange come about? The classic answer: through supply and demand. Got it? I can at least explain it to you technically:

Scenario 1: A buyer makes a bid for ten shares at 10 EUR each. A seller is willing to sell ten shares at the market price or at best (no matter at what price).

The transaction for ten shares is settled at 10 EUR, and the market price is 10 EUR.

Scenario 2: A buyer is looking for eight shares market or cheapest (no matter at what price). A seller is willing to sell 15 shares at 11 EUR each. The transaction is settled for eight shares at 11 EUR, and the market price is 11 EUR. The seller is left with seven shares until another buyer is found.

Scenario 3: A buyer submits a bid for ten shares at 10 EUR, and a seller is willing to sell 15 shares at 11 EUR each. Nothing happens. The price that was achieved at the last transaction (perhaps scenario 1) remains the current stock market price. If there are no transactions in one given day, the stock exchange might publish a theoretical price at noon or at the end of the day. In this case, 10.5 EUR, although no trading has taken place at this price.

There is not only one potential buyer or seller, but hundreds on each side with different expectations in terms of the number of shares and price (limits). I will spare the paper to print the order book of a stock exchange even if you plan to become a price setter (the so-called lead broker) at a stock exchange. I must tell you that for many years, a computer has been doing it.

What does the current share price tell?

The share price multiplied by the number of existing shares of the company indicates the stock market value, the so-called market capitalisation. If I want to buy the company as a whole, I will, theoretically, have to spend the equivalent of its market capitalisation to buy up all the shares. However, in reality, it looks different. As soon as I start buying shares from a company in significant quantities, I will quickly run out of sellers who will sell me the securities at a reasonable price. Besides that, I am required by regulation to announce certain thresholds (e.g., 10%) that I hold in the company so that I don't secretly collect all the available shares.

I therefore either have to find sellers who hold large blocks of shares and make a lucrative offer to buy their shares, or I can make a takeover offer to all shareholders. This offer should be so lucrative (e.g., 30% above the current share price) that as many investors as possible will agree to the offer because, if they don't, they might have to wait many years for a 30% share price gain.

However, for the buyer, it must be worth it to spend the market capitalisation + 30%, because nobody throws away money. There are several reasons: A company wants to grow by acquiring another to become the largest and most powerful company in its industry. This could mean future profits for the acquirer that recoup the purchase price.

In theory, the share price shows the value of the company, but no one really knows if this is correctly assessed (fair value). Analysts attempt to determine the fair value using mathematical models (e.g., discounted cash flow), but they are based on profit expectations for the next few years. You can imagine that it is hardly possible to predict the exact profits in four or five years. Hence the analyses and, above all, the price targets should be viewed with caution.

Nevertheless, I prefer reading the analyses because they often provide a good insight into the current situation of a company. And who likes to study the balance sheets themselves or has the chance to talk to the head of a company personally to get to the heart of the matter? Analysts have these opportunities. Analysts can't foresee the future (even though some may believe they can), but they can identify and point out opportunities and risks for the company.

So what do the current share prices express? The average opinion of the current value of the market capitalisation (remember market capitalisation divided by issued shares equals the share price). There are market participants who think that the market capitalisation is too low. They will tend to buy the shares. Those who think it is too high will sell the share (if they own it) or avoid it. If the average of all potential investors finds that the market capitalisation is higher than the current price indicates (i.e., not fairly valued), the share price will continue to rise until the supposed fair value is reached.

The dividends

What should be the reason to invest in stocks when it is so difficult to estimate the future profits of my chosen companies and I cannot necessarily bet on price gains? The profit sharing, the so-called dividends.

If a company makes a profit, it makes an important decision once a year. It can choose to keep the profits within the company to be able to invest without borrowing expensive outside capital. This is often the case with young stock corporations that are growing strongly. Alternatively, it can also distribute the profits or parts thereof to the shareholders. The stock corporation then decides at the shareholders' meeting that all shareholders receive a dividend payment for each share they hold.

Example: You hold 1,000 shares in XYZ AG. The share price is currently at 20 EUR. The company decides to pay a dividend of 0.50 EUR. You receive 500 EUR (0.5 EUR times 1 000 shares).

That is a 5% dividend yield on your current investment. But is this a profit for you? Not at first. Otherwise, it would be very easy to buy shares the day before the annual general meeting, cash in the money, and then sell the shares again.

With the payment of 0.50 EUR, the share price will also fall by half a euro. This is because the money is no longer within the company and is worth less due to the dividend paid out. What you have received in dividends has been taken away from you in the value of the shares. A zero-sum game, but one in which you have secured money that now belongs to you, even if the corporation unexpectedly goes bankrupt the day after tomorrow and the share price is at rock bottom.

As a rule, however, the company will continue to make profits, sometimes more and sometimes less. This in turn benefits the share price, so that the dividend discount is quickly recouped in the share price. If this game is repeated every year, eventually you will have received more dividend payments than you initially paid for the shares. That means you have the possibility to earn money with shares in the long term without being dependent on their actual performance or suffering if a company goes bankrupt after 30 years or so. It may not sound very exciting to wait 20 years, but companies are trying to constantly increase their profits and thus their dividends steadily. In practice, this can look like this:

Example: In 2010, Allianz AG paid a dividend of 4.10 EUR. After that, Allianz has continuously tried to increase the dividend, and in 2020 it was 9.60 EUR.
The share price in 2010 was approximately 78.8 EUR. After ten years, you would have received 71.25 EUR back via dividend payments. Fortunately, the share price was still at 157.89 EUR.

I can be honest; I don't have to sell you anything. If I had started the calculation in the year 2000, the dividend would have also increased continuously (it was 1.25 EUR at that time). However, the share price was so high due to the stock market hype at that time (around 400 EUR) that in 2020 it would not have even reached the dividend payments and the share price together. With the current level of dividends, you will have to wait 30 years. That is the burden of buying something too expensive.

The real fun begins when you didn't buy too expensively, your invested money is paid after 20 years with dividends, and at that point it is risk-free (you have already earned your money) and the share price has risen or at least has not fallen. In case you bought cheaply, you don't even have to wait 20 years. Unfortunately, I cannot tell you when a stock is 'cheap,' but at least I can show you a strategy later on so that you don't buy something too expensive.

Bonds

Fixed income, bonds, debt securities - so many terms

When it comes to bonds, there are many terms: bonds, debt securities, annuities, fixed income - and they all mean the same thing. They are generic terms for loans that are issued in the form of a security (technically: securitised) and give a return.

When a company or government wants to borrow on the capital market rather than from a bank (we are talking about EUR 250 - EUR 500 million), investment banks offer debtors the issuance of a bond:

Example: BMW wanted to borrow money on 11.01.2021 for EUR 500 million for twelve years on the capital market. An investment bank took up the matter and researched at what interest rate potential investors would be willing to lend the money. In other words, whether the bond would be bought at a price of approximately 100 (nominal). After positive feedback, the bank created a security, and after advertising and talking directly to possible investors, on January 11, 2021, bids were received from investors. Enough money was raised in the process, as the bond was launched with an annual interest promise of 0.2% for the next twelve years, along with the obligation to repay the invested money to the bondholder at the end of the term.

Please forgive me for anticipating some of the details already; I will explain them to you in more detail below.

The issue with the market interest rate

The entire financial market revolves around interest rates. Not only bonds, where it is obvious, but also real estate, stocks, and currencies are influenced by interest rates. Interests compensate the creditor in that he gives up his own capital for a certain period of time and during the time it is lent, he is not able to invest it and thus cannot increase it. The amount of interest is a science in itself. Let us take a look at the process. If you put your money privately in an account, you probably won't worry about the risk of default on the call money as long as it is covered by deposit insurance. After all, for you, it is largely risk-free. Incidentally, this is one reason why the interest rate hardly differs among call money providers.

If your money is not so safe because you give it to a foreign bank with little or no security, you will receive a higher interest rate. After all, giving money to a bank like that comes with a risk, and you want to have this risk rewarded. Usually, you can withdraw your overnight money within one day, which makes it flexible. If you put your money into a time deposit, you can't make flexible withdrawals as your money is tied up for longer. To compensate for the lack of flexibility, you may charge a higher interest rate as compensation.

There is such a thing as the market interest rate, but its exact value can only be determined for a maximum lending period of one night. Certainly, you have heard of the so-called prime rate. This is the interest rate set by the central bank; in Europe, this is the European Central Bank; in the US, it is the Federal Reserve Board, or short FED. For this interest rate, banks can invest their surplus money, but only for one night. Time deposits are not issued by the European Central Bank. Since the central bank is considered a safe haven for money, no one will be able to take on debt for less interest than the prime rate because then the potential creditor would rather give his money to the ECB.

When it comes to the market interest rate, which would have to be paid risk-free over a longer period of time, it is impossible to determine its value exactly. This is where the financial market acts (i.e., banks trade among themselves). Assumptions about interest rate developments have an influence, and everybody closely monitors what the others are doing. In the end, the level of the market interest rate is the average of what all investors are willing to pay at the moment for a given term (the same game as with stock prices).

The risk premium

Lending your money to a company comes with a risk. If you acquire a bond and the borrower becomes insolvent before the end of the term, you may have received a few interest payments; however, the large repayment sum at the end of the term does not materialise or is only a small amount (depending on the insolvency estate). No company in the world is safe from bankruptcy, not even Apple, Amazon, or Google. As a rule, all it takes are a few strategic mistakes on the part of the company's management, and to err is human. That is why the bond interest rate is calculated not only based on the market interest rate but also includes a risk premium or credit spread. The spread is based on the risk, which is naturally higher for a highly indebted airline than that of a conservative acting and less debt-laden energy supplier.

When I write about risk premiums, I inevitably also have to deal with ratings from rating agencies. There are agencies that analyse the risk of a debtor and grade it with a letter based on the U.S. school system. This is because the largest agencies (S&P, Moodys, Fitch) are from the U.S. The grades used are as follows: A (preferably three of them, i.e., AAA) stands for low risk, B is already dangerous, and C stands for extreme risk. With a D, the bankruptcy vulture has already struck.

I personally do not prefer ratings when making investment decisions, as rating agencies are paid by the debtor for their analyses, and the speed with which the rating assessments change is far too volatile. It is better to use credit spreads for your evaluation; they express an independent risk assessment (namely that of the market) and are always up-to-date. Unfortunately, it is much easier for private investors to find the ratings on relevant financial websites than the spreads. And fund managers often have to look at ratings too because their backers may have imposed restrictions on them, such as 'do not buy bonds with a rating lower than BBB.' This is also because rating rules are much easier to contractually define than credit spread rules.

The bond price

If you see the price of a bond and it says 99.87 EUR, it does not mean that you are paying 99.87 EUR for a bond. Bonds are not bought in units but in nominal amounts. So you buy 10,000 EUR nominal at the price of 99.87 EUR and have to effectively pay 9,987 EUR (10,000 x 0.9987). If the bond were priced at 115 EUR, you would have to pay 11,500 EUR for 10,000 EUR in nominal value (10,000 x 1.15). At the end of the term, you will receive the bond back at a price of 100, which means that for 10,000 nominal you also get 10,000 EUR paid out.

In addition, there is interest. Therefore, it can make sense to buy a bond that is above 100 even if you lose money at the end of the term. If the bond falls from 110 to 100 at the time of purchase, this is a price loss, but if you earned more than 10% in interest during the term, your investment may have paid off after all.

In the US, bonds quotes regular in points and thirty-seconds of a point, not in decimal form. If you see a bond price of 100.75 for a U.S. Treasury Note (government bonds), it means 100.23 in decimal (75/32).

Special forms of bonds

The classic bond is the fixed-rate bond, which pays a fixed interest rate once a year and is repaid in full at the end of the term at a price of 100. Under certain circumstances, these bonds may contain a clause that gives the debtor the right to cancel the bond on a certain date. These are known as callable bonds. Callable means that the bond is immediately redeemed at 100, and from that point on no more interest has to be paid. It is annoying if you have just paid 130 for the bond and tomorrow it is redeemed for 100 without you having received much interest. That's why issuing callable bonds often subject to restrictions that allow early redemption after a certain period at the earliest or at certain times.

Covered bonds are similar to bonds except that they are collateralised with real estate, aircraft, or ships, for example. Here, two things are liable: the bank that issued the covered bond and the pawn itself (which, by the way, was financed by the covered bond).

This is what makes a covered bond so safe; it regularly receives AAA ratings and therefore hardly yields any interest. ABS (Asset Backed Securities) are also covered bonds, but without liability on the part of the issuing bank. A book could be written about this topic alone. The subtype of ABS is the MBS (Mortgage-Backed Securities), the root cause of the financial market crisis of 2007-2008, i.e., a security backed by real estate loans, plus tranches, which are risk gradations in the

ABS with different interest rates. If the real estate loans behind it are bad, which nobody knows about, and all the major banks hold these papers, a huge investment bank like Lehman Brothers can become insolvent.

Then there are zero bonds, which are bonds without an interest coupon. They are issued at 90%, for example, run for five years, and are repaid at 100%. The creditor is remunerated by the price gain.

Floaters are bonds with a variable interest rate; they are linked to an official market interest rate. The market interest rate together with the total interest rate that is paid to you on a regular basis. At the end of the term, the bond is repaid at 100. For a long time, the prevailing market interest rates in the euro area were negative. If the market interest rate and risk premium together are negative, fortunately nothing is taken away from you. The total interest is 0.

There are many other designs like convertibles, contingent convertibles, and contingent notes, which I won't mention here because some of them are not available to private investors anyway. However, you may be offered an investment fund that deals with these types of securities.

Practical tips

Bonds are the most important asset class for institutional investors. This is where the largest investment volume flows in as one can generate regular income with manageable price risks, and they can therefore become profitable quickly. Almost all of these transactions take place outside a stock exchange with investment banks acting as intermediaries between buyer and seller. This is similar to the secondhand car market.

As a private investor, you need an exchange. If you type 'bond finder' into a search engine, you will find a page on the internet where you can look at potential bonds and borrow them.

When analysing what the bond may bring you as a return within a year, it is best to use the indicated yield. In addition to the interest rate, it also includes the purchase price into the calculation because the bond, which may currently cost 110, will only be repaid at 100 in the end.

Once you have decided on a security, note down the security identification number that you will need to purchase the bond from your bank.

Commodities

Futures

I would have liked to spare you from writing about financial market instruments, which are almost exclusively used by professional investors. But if you invest indirectly with certificates or so-called ETCs (more on this later), because in most cases you do not buy the actual investment object directly, you should understand what actually happens with your money. This is mostly the case with commoditics. Nothing is more annoying than betting on the right horse and gaining nothing.

Futures are a financial instrument that invests in something - we call it the underlying asset - without the need to own it. If I buy futures, I do not have to pay anything. However, I would have to pay the price losses every evening if the underlying asset falls. On the other hand, I also get paid the profits every evening if the underlying asset rises. Products whose values or payouts depend on underlying assets are called derivatives. In addition to futures, the derivatives world also includes options and swaps.

All derivatives have one thing in common: they come with a maturity date. At the end of their term, futures will be worth as much as their corresponding underlying asset. Before that, there are usually deviations. It must be taken into account somewhere that no money is needed to buy the underlying asset directly; otherwise, nobody would buy stocks anymore, for example, and only invest in futures. The greater the advantage of not having to buy the underlying asset and the further away the maturity date is, the greater the premium of the futures.

Incidentally, it may also be that the future has no premium but is cheaper in price than the underlying asset.
Example: You want to buy the futures of the XYZ share, which is currently quoted at 100 EUR. If the future still has three months to run and you receive exactly the underlying security at the end of the term, the future will then be quoted below 100 EUR if the share pays a dividend of, say, 5 EUR within the next three months. On the day of the dividend payment, the assets are now worth 5 EUR less per share because the company has distributed parts of its own assets. If the share price falls, the future holder must accept a loss because he will not receive the exemplary 5 EUR on is account as compensation. Therefore, the future is quoted below the current share price to compensate for this disadvantage.

The example shows why derivatives cannot exist without a maturity date. Only if there is a maturity date is a fair calculation possible (savings in credit interest, known dividend payments). This shows the advantage that the derivative holder has over the direct investor. In practice, there are futures on an underlying asset with several maturities, and new specifications are brought to market at regular intervals. When a future is about to expire and an investor wishes to remain invested, he sells the expiring futures and at the same time buys a contract with a longer maturity. This process is called rolling.

A future can also be sold without having been bought beforehand. With this minus position (technical term 'short position'), you would get money every evening when the underlying asset fell. What sounds like wild speculation is very often applied by investors to hedge their investments in uncertain times without having to sell all the underlying assets. If I sell two DAX®futures, I am two contracts short. If I sell another two futures, I will be four contracts short. If I then buy four futures, I am flat. In case I buy three more, I am three contracts long and betting on rising prices.

Certificates / ETC

If private investors want to invest in commodities via securities, they have, in general, two options. First option: You purchase a fund that invests in commodities. In this case, you will always have a basket of commodities, never just one, because a fund must be diversified. It may bet on several horses of the same breed, but never on only one.

The second possibility would be to buy the so-called obligation of an issuer, which is usually a bank. You automatically enter a contract with someone who agrees to give you a payout on certain terms. These obligations are usually called 'certificates.'

Example: You buy a certificate from an investment bank that promises you a profit if the price of gold rises. If gold rises by 1%, your certificate also increases in value by about 1%. However, it also loses 1% if gold falls by 1%.

When it comes to the design of the certificates, the banks' imagination has no limits - it's a bit like a betting shop. There you can bet on the number of corners, the number of goals between the 65th and the 80th minute, or whether there will be a penalty kick which will also be missed. With the certificates, it is the same. Special payouts are made when price thresholds are reached or, in another case, if they are not reached. Double profit when the price of the underlying asset falls? No problem at all!

Less exciting but quite practical is the fact that certificates also give you the possibility to invest in or participate in commodities of any kind, quite often even without a maturity date. You can cancel the bond at any time by reselling the certificates. When you sell shares on the stock exchange, an unknown market participant buys them. If you sell certificates, the bank usually buys them back.

Important: Banks do not bet against you. Banks secure themselves on the financial market against the obligation to pay out the certificates to you.

Example: You buy a certificate that brings you profits if silver falls. The issuing bank looks at how many other customers have also bought these certificates and calculates how much silver futures it has to sell in order not to suffer a loss if the commodity then really falls. It will then position itself in the market accordingly, which comes at a certain cost. The bank's profits depend on how efficiently it does that.

Unfortunately, with certificates, in addition to choosing the right investment, you also have to consider a negative aspect: the issuer risk. If the issuer goes bankrupt, you may not get any money back if you try to sell the securities. It is easier said than done to check out the creditworthiness of the issuer before buying the certificate and to monitor it on an ongoing basis. Refer to the previous chapter on bonds in the section on the risk premium to be able to at least somewhat assess the risk.

ETCs (Exchange Traded Commodities) are also debt securities and therefore come with an issuer risk. They can also be used to invest in individual commodities, but they are better collateralised than certificates. Ideally, they are physically linked to the commodity they track, which is usually the case with precious metals, ETCs. In the case of an oil ETC, it is possible that no oil was bought but bonds, and they still give you the performance of the black gold. How does this work? I will briefly introduce you to the world of swaps. These are rather part of the bigger basics of the stock exchange, but it does not harm to take a look at the risks involved in these financial products in advance.

Swaps

The term 'swap' stands for 'exchange,' and on the financial market it means an exchange transaction. There are many swaps on the market; these are used by professional investors and are not suitable for private investors as they involve an unlimited risk of loss. In any case, swap transactions are concluded with minimum sums of between one and five million euros and require special contracts (known as master agreements, e.g., ISDA) between two swap partners. The following things can be exemplified by two market participants (one of them is usually an investment bank):

Example 1: Party A receives a fixed interest on a volume of exemplarily EUR 50 million and pays Party B a variable interest rate in return. The swap is called an IRS (Interest Rate Swap).
Example 2: Party A receives EUR 5 million from Party B when a certain company goes bankrupt and pays Party B an insurance premium. This swap is called a CDS (Credit Default Swap).

For us, the private investors, the total return swap is much more interesting because it indirectly has something to do with our potential investments. It can be described as a 'full performance swap.' Here, party A pays a fee or an interest rate to party B. In return, party B must pay the gains from an underlying asset. If the development is negative, A must compensate B for the losses. Does it sound illogical that A has to pay for profits and losses equally and pays an additional fee while B loses nothing at all?

Let's look at typical underlying assets for such a swap: commodities and indices. Buying commodities yourself, storing them, or even having access to the market for commodities is barely possible, even for professional market participants such as investment funds. Even with a stock index, it can be difficult for professionals to copy the performance accurately at any given time, even though the purchase of shares is not a problem in itself. The difficulty is having the right weighting of the shares at any time. Fortunately, there are investment banks that specialise in providing the exact desired payout profile, albeit for a fee. But the bank itself will also hedge its bets. Ideally, it will find another market participant that wants to hedge against a price drop in commodities.

Example 3: Party A speculates on rising copper prices and concludes a total return swap on copper with Party B, an investment bank. Party C, on the other hand, wants to protect itself against falling prices and also enters into a total return swap with Party B but with a different payout profile. Here, party B pays money to party C if copper falls, and party C pays money to party B if copper rises.

You find the example very contrived and might think that it is a huge coincidence, or at least very theoretical, that A and C have opposite interests and want to trade exactly the same volume with the same maturity. You are right, but an investment bank has hundreds or thousands of speculators and hedgers among its customers. The bank will try to even out the different interests as best it can. If the bank does not succeed on a one-to-one basis, it can always hedge by simply buying the underlying asset itself. In doing so, the profit for the bank will be diminished; however, it will never be dependent on how the price of an underlying asset develops. As the saying goes, 'the bank always wins.'

What happens if the investment bank fails or, in other words, when it goes insolvent? Basically, as an investor, I lose out because if the bank is insolvent, it won't pay out anything to me. But there are safeguards.

The first safeguard mechanism is that profits and losses are offset on a regular basis. In the circles of experts, this is known as a 'reset.' You may be familiar with it as a button on electrical devices, and this is somewhat comparable. In the case of the device, it goes back to the default settings, and it can start all over again. In the case of a swap, the pending profit or loss that has accrued up to that point between the two contracting parties is paid at regular intervals. The profit and loss statement starts all over again, and money that was paid through a reset can no longer be lost through insolvency.

For example, if a reset is performed every Friday and a swap partner becomes insolvent on the Thursday before, a maximum of the profit since the last reset (the Friday before) is lost.

Second security mechanism: A collateral agreement is drawn. This is an agreement between the swap partners that a pledge (collateral) will be exchanged among each other in order to secure pending profits. If party A incurs a loss that exceeds a previously agreed threshold, it must pay the collateral to party B. If the loss turns into a profit, Party B must offset it. If one of the parties becomes insolvent in the meantime, the collateral may be realised if any profits cannot be paid.

Why not just make daily resets and deposit collateral before any pending profit or loss occurs? That means that there would indeed be no risk, and this is exactly how futures that are traded on an exchange are traded. There, the collateral is called initial margin (money you have to deposit at the beginning) and the resets are called variation margin (money you have to pay or get after each trading day). But this one hundred percent security comes at a cost.

Every payment stream, whether caused by a reset or collateral, must be calculated, checked, and instructed. The counterparties must ensure on a daily basis that they have sufficient funds available. This leads to a buffer being held in reserve, and this safety buffer cannot be invested. Anyone who buys a certificate or funds using swaps wants to pay as little ongoing fees as possible. Therefore, it is important to find a sensible balance between cost and security.

What does all this have to do with commodities? When you buy a certificate or fund that allows you to make a commodity investment, you are, in most cases, buying a construct that does not actually buy the commodities itself. You would rather buy a construct that gives you the swap-based result of a commodity investment. It is possible that you are buying a commodity fund that is full of bonds and does not have a single commodity in it. The bonds are then used to provide collateral to a swap partner, which in turn provides the commodity result.

It can also happen that shares or bond funds are swap-based. The opposite of swap-based is physically replicated (backed by real assets). Why commodities are rarely physically replicated will be discussed below for the individual types of commodities.

Precious metals - suitability as an investment object

Metals that do not rust are called precious metals. Among the most famous are gold, silver, platinum, and palladium. These can be stored easily and are therefore also suitable as physical investments. By standardisation and classification, like bars,

Krugerrand, etc., it is fairly easy to estimate how much the objects you may be holding in your hands are worth.

Is it suitable as an investment object? This is where the experts argue. The following applies to all commodities: They do not spawn, they do not yield interest, neither a dividend. If your goal is to generate price gains and pay interest on your investment, commodities lose out on the latter point. Worse: Storing them (safely) costs money, more than with securities.

What about potential price gains? For this to happen, demand would have to constantly exceed supply. Here, the commodity precious metal has an advantage over food as a commodity because it is finite, which can lead to a shortage of supply and thus to rising prices. However, precious metals can be easily recycled. For a supply shortage of gold and the other precious metals is necessary that a new product or even an industry emerge that will trigger a lasting demand. An example was the invention of the cell phone and the resulting demand for 'rare-earths,' since these are needed to manufacture the cell phone and everyone in the world wanted to have one. Precious metals have a unique selling proposition that can lead to price gains: their store of value.

Gold, in particular, is considered a crisis currency. Whenever there is a major crisis in the world, the precious metals start to rise in price as they are considered a safe haven. No matter whether an economic crisis is looming and stocks are falling, the spectre of inflation or bond prices fall, the precious metals remain steadfast. It would be immoral to buy gold and silver, hoping that many wars will break out. In any case, this speculation would not be particularly promising since a certain expectation that there will always be crises is already reflected in market rates. On the stock market, it is always the probable future that is traded. That also goes for commodity exchanges.

Forms of investment

There are four ways for private investors to invest in precious metals.

Option 1:

You physically buy the metals and put them in a vault. There are various providers (e.g., in Germany: Ophirum, Degussa Gold, Pro Aurum) where you can buy the precious metals, and in some places there are even vending machines for these metals. The margin between purchase and sale price is however enormous. If you have just purchased an ingot, the commodity has to rise enormously in order to make a profit.

Option 2:

You buy a certificate for gold. There are a variety of certificate issuers that sell securities which give you an almost identical representation of the price development of the desired commodity. The difference between the buying and selling price is limited, but there is an annual fee which reduces possible profits or aggravates losses. If the certificate issuer becomes insolvent, you might face a total loss. If you plan to hold the certificate for 30 years, the annual fee will really hurt. The longer you hold these certificates, the more likely it is that the fees will suffer a loss. Maybe we don't have to assume the worst, and an issuer is simply taken over by another company. In this case, you have an issuer, and if necessary, they will terminate the certificate for you (this is stated in the small print of the prospectus that it is allowed to do so). When a certificate is terminated, you get paid what the security is worth on the date of termination. However, it is annoying if you are in the loss zone or if your investment was planned for 30 years.

In the short to medium term, it is conceivable to use certificates, above all, to bet on falling prices. In the long run, you have to live with the scenarios I have described above.

If you decide in favour of certificates, use the certificate special form ETC. Here, the insolvency protection is greater since the actual commodity is deposited with the issuer for hedging purposes. Not one hundred percent, but at least a large part of it.

Option 3:

You buy a commodity ETF. ETFs are funds and must be diversified. Therefore, an ETF cannot bet on a single commodity. Beware, trap! Type in a search engine gold or silver ETF'. You will be offered lists of ETFs on single commodities, and if you look closer, they are ETCs in the end. Here the good name 'ETF' (it is insolvency-proof) is misused to attract customers, but in the end, you don't keep one in your portfolio.

But there is a halfway acceptable solution. Gold, silver, platinum, and the like are strongly correlated. When gold rises in price, the other precious metals usually rise as well. Sometimes one rises stronger than the other. This makes sense because, in times of crisis, for example, all the precious metals often become more expensive. Even if one of the precious metals booms due to strong industrial demand, the others follow suit. Perhaps not all to the same extent, but if you have an ETF that invests across all precious metals, you have a reasonable commodity exposure. You don't even have to think about whether you should rather bet on gold or silver.

Option 4:

You buy an ETF on precious metals companies. Companies that profit from rising precious metal prices are primarily the mines, many of whom are listed on the stock exchange, and their profits rise many times over when precious metal prices increase in price. Actually, it does not matter if the mine you are investing in only produces gold and the price of silver increases. The correlation (see possibility 3 above) benefits the gold miners. Since there are so many public companies whose wealth depends on gold, there are now plenty of indices, and where there is an index, an ETF is usually not far behind. The indices and associated ETFs are called 'Gold Miners' or 'Gold Bugs.' Beware: Even though it may seem at first glance to be the best of both worlds - shares (which usually rise in the long run) and commodities – it is not a standard stock investment. Mining stocks are a kind of its own. Political turmoil, adverse legislation, currency fluctuations, and dependence on one commodity make this investment very risky. An index, and therefore the ETF that tracks it, can fall sharply and never recover. If political tensions remain absent and commodity prices rise, gold bugs will rise disproportionately. For speculators who are betting on a short-term rise in commodities, this is an exciting situation. For those who want to invest their money in a reasonably safe and balanced investment, it is less suitable.

Risks

Currency risk: Regardless of whether you invest physically or with securities in precious metals, you should be aware that these commodities are traded in U.S. dollars on the world market. If gold costs 1,500 USD and the EUR/USD exchange rate rises from 1.20 to 1.25 (thus the dollar becomes weaker), the gold is no longer worth 1,250 EUR but 1,200 EUR.

This is usually not so bad because gold is an excellent way to store value for a reason. Therefore, the price of gold will start to rise and compensate for this shortfall. Just because the dollar weakens, it does not automatically make gold shine less beautifully. But if you invest in gold and tomorrow read joyfully in the newspaper that gold has risen, look at the exchange rate before you rejoice, and don't be surprised why the commodity ETF or gold ETC didn't move.

If you are invested in gold bugs and the currencies of the countries in which most of the mining companies are located devalue, the story is a different one. Australia is number one when it comes to mining. Second place goes to Russia, and third is South Africa. The Russian Ruble and South African Rand certainly carry a greater currency risk than the Australian Dollar.

Storage costs: Storing precious metals costs money for insurance, a vault and transportation. If the prices of precious metals run sideways for years (I don't even want to think about falling prices), the costs will hurt your ETC, certificate, or ETF. There is no interest or dividend. The price of precious metals has to go up for the investment to be worthwhile in the end.

Energy / Industrial metals / Food

Raw materials: energy (e.g., oil, gas), industrial metals (e.g. lead, copper), and agriculture (e.g., wheat, corn, coffee) have one thing in common. They are difficult to store, cannot be locked in a vault, and have to be represented by derivatives (mostly futures) by fund companies or certificates. This is a heavy burden, so heavy that it becomes a serious problem for private investors. But let's take it one step at a time.

Non-renewable raw materials

Non-renewable raw materials are becoming scarcer as consumption increases; a classic is oil. This means that a certain supply shortage is on the horizon and promises to be a safe investment. However, from an economic point of view, the pressure to replace the raw material with other (better and cheaper available materials) rises constantly. This can be done faster for industrial metals than for oil and gas. The lack of renewability of raw materials is therefore not a guarantee for infinitely increasing raw material prices.

Renewable raw materials

This is where morality strikes especially hard. By investing in wheat, for example, your first appearance on the market will be as a buyer. An ever-increasing demand on the market drives up commodity prices and makes vital agricultural products more expensive for people, who therefore might have to face hunger because they cannot afford the food price anymore. Investing in wood raises prices and motivates others to cut down more trees. For this reason, there are commodity indices that contain the suffix 'ex agriculture,' meaning they exclude agricultural products.

Regardless of morality, renewable raw materials also have one economically plausible characteristic: they are cyclical. When commodity prices are high, they are cultivated intensively, and the warehouses fill up. At some point, the prices go down, the warehouses empty out, and the time comes when shortages strike again. For short-term investors, it is certainly interesting to take advantage of this cycle; however, this also carries dangers and is something more for advanced investors.

Risks

What else can go wrong with commodities apart from precious metals? I'll get into the long-term problems later; let me point out the more short-term pitfalls first:

1. Commodity prices on foodstuffs tend to be highly exaggerated and often experience volatile price movements. The commodity exchanges therefore have a mechanism called 'limit up' and 'limit down,' which means that trading in the commodity can be suspended at any time if there are large fluctuations during the day. During my career, I have experienced that on several days in a row there was a 'limit up' for wheat. Anyone who then had a wheat certificate could not sell it to take the profits because, without prices on the stock exchange, there is no price for the certificate. That's somewhere in the fine print. If there is no price on the stock exchange for a longer period, a certificate issuer could, of course, determine a price only to the best of its knowledge and belief.

2. Commodities are quoted in USD, and some are also quoted in GBP, but never in EUR. There is therefore always a currency risk to be considered.

3. There is no 100 percent insolvency-proof way to invest in commodities. ETCs are better secured than certificates, but especially in the case of energy, industrial metals, or foodstuff, they cannot be physically backed by the respective commodity.

Contango and backwardation

Forward curves

Contango and backwardation are terms that are closely associated with commodity trading and have an enormous impact on yields. Contango and backwardation are so-called forward curves.

When someone buys a future on a commodity, at the end of the future's term, the buyer commits to buy a certain quantity of a certain quality of the commodity in question and to pay the current market price. Whoever sells the future (i.e., has a short position) must deliver the commodity. This mechanism ensures that the future is fairly priced. If it were too cheap, real commodity traders (i.e., not speculators) would only buy their commodities via futures and not on the market. Excess demand for the future causes its price to rise, and soon it is no longer too cheap. This market mechanism only works because a future has a maturity date at which it is settled. Therefore, futures can never run indefinitely.

Most futures traders are not commodity traders. No one is interested in getting deliveries of bunches of wheat, pork belly halves, or oil barrels. For this reason, a futures position is closed before the expiration date. Whoever bought five wheat futures which expire on day X will sell these five wheat futures before that day X. He has thus closed out his position. Whoever has sold ten oil futures and is therefore short ten contracts will buy ten contracts before day X to close out his position.

What happens if the closing is forgotten? It is the biggest fear, even for institutional investors, to get into this scenario. I once heard from an investment bank that they have departments that take care of just such a scenario and help investors out of the jam. But this will certainly not be a free service.

What happens if an investor wants to be invested in the commodity even after the current future has expired? Before a future expires on day X, there will already be a future Y, which will run for three months longer than X. If I sell X and buy Y at the same time, I have a constant investment. The simultaneous purchase and sale of contracts with different expiration terms is called rolling.

The roll loss and its effect

Let's assume we buy a future with six months to run. By doing that, we save ourselves the trouble of physically storing the commodity, insuring it, and even having to pay for it today. We actually don't have to do all that until the expiration date, that is, if we haven't rolled the future. The physical commodity trader has the storage and insurance costs, and he already had to invest his money, which he would have gotten interest on elsewhere. As I already mentioned, most commodities are quoted in USD. In the USA, there have been no negative interest rates so far, so there will be a financing interest rate as a surcharge.

If I agree with a commodity trader that we will do the deal in four months' time at today's price (that is all a future really is), the trader will take a surcharge on today's price. This represents the storage and financing costs. The longer the contract runs, the higher the markup. This means that future X, which may expire in one month, is cheaper than future Y, which matures in four months' time. With increasing time, the future becomes cheaper and cheaper. This curve is called a contango.

If you hold a future on a commodity and on the market the price for the corresponding commodity does not change, the value of your future will decrease every day. You are paying the storage costs that you actually do not have. To book a profit, future sales must therefore increase more than the daily storage costs. If you roll into the future, it becomes much more expensive (it runs longer).

Now we come to the point where you will find a lot of nonsense written about this topic. The same goes for numerous publications on video channels: the 'roll loss.'

Example number 1:

The old future is sold for 100 and the new one is bought for 120. There is an immediate loss of 20.

Example number 2:

The certificate issuer sells the old future for 100 and receives only 0.83 percent of the future, which costs 120. After all, he had not been able to earn more money from the sale of the old company. After rolling the future, the certificate only increases by 0.83% if the commodity increases by 1%.

When a future is bought or sold, there is no transfer of money. If I buy in the afternoon at 100, and the closing price on the same day is 102, the exchange will pay me 2 as profit. If last night the closing price of the futures was 105 and today, I sell it during the day at 103, I incur a loss of 2. When I roll, I buy and sell at the same time. If I have a profit on one side, I have a loss on the other, and by the same amount! There is no rolling loss; the term is misleading. In the meantime, the term 'rolling effect' is becoming more and more accepted, but there is still no immediate effect due to rolling.

Why does the certificate issuer change the participation rate (mostly to my disadvantage)? because the issuer does not want to influence the certificate price by rolling. If he leaves the participation rate at 100%, he will have to set the price of the certificate upwards after the roll (the new future is more expensive). If he does that and I then buy the certificate before the roll of the issuer, then it jumps up and I sell. A risk-free profit for me - no bank in the world would go along with that. Does the bank then rip me off? No, it doesn't. It just does not explain it correctly, so the real reason isn't so obvious. For an issuer, holding a commodity future costs money expressed in contango. To make sure that the price of the certificate does not decrease constantly, participation is used. Through this, you do not have any advantage or disadvantage by buying or selling at a very specific time.

Backwardation: a buying argument?

Is it possible that a future with a longer term is sometimes cheaper than one with a shorter term? Yes, this is called backwardation. The price of the future increases the closer we get to the end of the term.

How can that be? With commodities, sometimes you know exactly when they are going to rise or fall, and as long as all market participants have the knowledge, that is priced into the futures.

Example: It's 10 p.m. on Tuesday night, and you want to make an agreement with a gas station lessee to fill up with 50 the next day, and you want to fix the price for it already. At the moment, the gas station has the expensive night tariff on its price board, and a litre of gas just costs 2 EUR. Will you fix the price for the litre at 2 EUR with the lessee or rather aim for 1.90 EUR? You know that the lessee sells the fuel at an expensive night tariff. The fuel future that you have just concluded with the lessee is in backwardation.

Whether in contango or backwardation, there is no situation that promises risk-free profits. The futures price curve is the result of available market information (interest rates, storage costs, and upcoming price-moving events) and mathematics.

The consequence for the long-term investment

Let me explain this tangle with contango more easily. Without futures at all: 'Investing in commodities always incurs storage costs. This must be paid by the investor and makes any long-term investment unprofitable unless it rises permanently.'

The ETC, ETF, or certificate industry tries to disguise this. They talk about 'enhanced' indexes that should optimise rolling costs. Therefore, you should know that there is no roll cost caused by forward curves at all. What has been optimised here is the timing of the futures rolls. You should not roll in the last second of the life of a future, not even weeks before (to make sure that the roll is not forgotten). This is because either the old future is not liquid (i.e., not enough market participants are trading it) or the new one is not. Therefore, there are optimal roll times when both futures are reasonably liquid.

It does not change anything in terms of storage costs. There have certainly been periods when commodities have risen for almost ten years at a time, and the storage costs have always come in. But there are also weak phases, and then it gets really bitter as you have storage costs and price losses.

Commodities don't pay interest or dividends. A company with constant costs but no earnings is very critical for long-term investment. With certificates, the magic quickly disappears looking at the participation rate. With ETCs and ETFs, storage costs are easier to work into the price as a negative effect.

Forward curves as a trading opportunity?

Trading and exploiting certain patterns are called trading. Often, these are short-term trades. If the commodities are mostly in contango, and consequently the difference between the future price and the real price becomes smaller on the expiration date, isn't there a way to make money with that? If you simply go short on the commodity (there are, of course, certificates for this), the storage costs come your way, but if the commodity rises, you are in the loss zone.

There is an index, CYD Market Neutral, that does the following: It shortens the expiring month and extends it into the future. That makes it market neutral, it doesn't matter if commodities go up or down for now. The effect exploited here is minimal and can barely cover the transaction costs; it is so minimal that the index is leveraged and gets the addition plus 5 (or more). Then the return already gets better; this goes well until there is a surprise backwardation. If you are then leveraged, the index goes down sharply in a very short time.

Conclusion for practice

Long-term commodity investing is difficult. Storage costs are priced into any type of vehicle, whether certificate, ETC, or ETF, and thus kill returns. Over the long term, a steady price increase is needed to cover the commodity-specific costs while still making a profit on the bottom line. In the case of certificates and ETCs, there is also the issuer risk, which is not negligible for an investment period of 20 or 30 years.

Physical investments would mitigate the storage costs, especially if someone has rented a safe deposit box somewhere. The high difference between buying and selling prices does not make physical investment a short- or medium-term bet. Those who do not trust central banks and governments can have precious metals physically added to their assets as a 'safe haven.' Then it has at least the purpose of pure value preservation; whether it leads to price gains, nobody knows; that would be speculation.

Away from precious metals, i.e., commodities that can at most be stored as a tank filling in the car or cellar, an investment is suitable for the short- to medium-term at most. But even here, there are risks involved; the price risk alone is enormous.

Commodities are cyclical; they can rise quite quickly and fall again at the same speed.

Do you still want to profit from increasingly scarce energy commodities? Then invest in companies that do not have the storage problem and profit from rising prices because they extract or resell the raw material. I won't mention a specific company here, but I can tell you that there are now ETFs not only on gold companies (gold bugs), but also on profiteers of future oil or water shortages.

Money market, foreign currencies

Savings account, call money, time deposit

The times when interest rates on savings books were over 3% are over for the time being. If those times come back, it will have such negative consequences for some European countries (state bankruptcies!) that it is hard to imagine that the ECB will ever allow interest rates to reach the level of 2008. It is not out of the question; however, if we have inflation well above 2%, they may have no other choice.

Overnight accounts exist nonetheless, and even if some of them do not pay any interest, they at least do not charge a negative interest rate for private individuals. In the institutional sector, it has long been the case that negative interest rates are charged on overnight deposits. Here, however, the deposits also start only at EUR 1 million . I myself have already had to invest EUR 1 billion of overnight money for investment funds. The call money banks could not do anything with the money, as a further investment with the ECB would have cost them penalty interest. By the way, an investment fund cannot park money directly with the ECB; only banks can do that.

Time deposits also made little sense. To capitalise on a positive euro interest rate, the term was simply too long and, in some cases, not even allowed for funds. Would you give your money to a fund that would then invest it at a negative interest rate?
Savings books, call money, and time deposits are so-called money market products; however, the savings book is only available to private investors. If you try to find a money market provider that still offers noticeable interest rates, the money is either not insolvency-proof or it is a temporary loss leader.

This should however not prevent you from holding money as an investment, albeit non-interest bearing. If you have to pull out of a long-term investment (e.g., stocks) because you need money for an unforeseen repair, it would be bitter to say goodbye to an investment that is just in the red but would have been a good long-term investment. In such cases, it's better to keep some money in reserve with little to no interest.

Money market funds

It used to be said of money market funds that they take advantage of their institutional status so that they get better interest rates on overnight deposits than private individuals. That's why they collect the money of private individuals, invest it collectively, and return the higher interest to their shareholders again. But sometimes the private investor has the privilege of getting better overnight deposit rates.

For money market funds to still exist, they must invest their money in short-dated bonds. These are also still considered money market products because there are almost no price fluctuations to be expected. However, since short-dated bonds now also yield negative returns if they are as safe as German government securities, it is inevitable that more risky securities have to be purchased. So, anyone buying a money market fund today is buying a bond fund with short-dated bonds, some of which are not particularly loss-proof. Take a look at the semiannual or annual report of a money market fund (you can find these on the common financial information sites) - you will be amazed.

Foreign exchange and the foreign interest rate

If there are negative (or low) interest rates in the euro area, then it is obvious to think about an investment in a foreign currency. You exchange EUR into USD and invest it in the American currency with a higher interest rate. Regardless of whether your bank allows you such an account model, you can also buy interest certificates which reflect exactly this investment idea for all possible currencies.

Regardless of which form of collecting foreign interest you choose; you bear the exchange rate risk. Rising interest rates strengthen currencies because the higher the interest rate, the greater the demand for the corresponding currency. If interest rates are (surprisingly) lowered, the currency weakens. If you hold a certificate or money in a foreign currency and interest rates are lowered, it becomes doubly bitter. There is subsequently less interest, and the invested money (or purchased certificate) is suddenly worth less due to the devaluation of the currency.

With bonds in foreign currencies, you have the same problem as with interest rate certificates: foreign currency risk and issuer risk. When you buy foreign currency, you are doing it either for speculation, for short-term trading, or as a hedge because you may be skeptical about the euro.

Real Estate, Ships, Media

Real estate, ships, or media do not have a number and are not traded on the stock exchange; hence, they do not fit into the multiplication tables of the stock exchange. There are funds, and if you buy them, they end up in your securities account. I am not an expert in these special fields, but nevertheless, I would like to share a few basics about funds.

Closed-end funds

A closed-end fund is used for project financing for which there is a business plan and a certain return is expected. For this, a capital company is founded, money is collected, a fixed number of share certificates are issued, and then the project starts. Real estate, ships, or forests are purchased; a film is financed; and hopes are pinned on high box office takings. During the project phase, the capital company does not want any money from you but you commit yourself not to take any money from the company during the project phase. The fund is not a special asset; in the event of the insolvency of the company or the failure of the project, your money is gone. You are facing a total loss!

Open funds

Real estate funds are often set up as open-ended real estate investment funds. You can buy and sell shares every day; in addition, the assets are safe from the insolvency of the fund company.

But what does the real estate fund manager do? He buys buildings, collects rent, and then sells the buildings again. If too many investors want to get out of the fund at the same time, he has a problem. While an equity fund manager can liquidate his entire fund in two to three days, a real estate fund manager can, a real estate manager cannot. He needs weeks and months, which is why he always has to have some money ready, but it must not be too much either because a high a cash buffer reduces the return.

If there is not enough money to redeem share certificates, the redemptions must be suspended, and you will not receive any money for an indefinite period of time! Liquidity is the biggest risk for the real estate fund owner.

Alternatives - practical tips

You want to get the asset class real estate into your portfolio without the liquidity risk of ETFs. Then, as with commodities, you can switch to shares. Because of the individual risk, an ETF is also the more reasonable option here; however, the price trend will not go from bottom left to top right, as is the case with real estate funds. It is and will remain an investment in equities.

Volatility

Volatility is an expression for the fluctuation in intensity of an item within a certain period of time. How can this be an asset class?

The option market

An option is a financial contract between two players. Party A agrees with party B that on a certain date they may buy (e.g., on the third Friday in October at 5 p.m.) a product (e.g., shares of XYZ) at a certain price (e.g., 150 EUR) from B. They may, but not must. If, at a certain time, share XYZ costs only 140 EUR, it does not make sense for A to acquire it via the option for 150 EUR. The option is worthless. The option had a value at the time it was agreed upon since no one could have known that the share would not rise above 150 EUR. Party A paid money to B as a premium for the option, and B did not have to pay anything for it in the end.

If the share had risen to 160 EUR, B would have had to buy the share on the market for that price just to deliver it to A at 150 EUR. A loss of just under 10 EUR would have been incurred, somewhat mitigated by the premium that A paid to B.

There are what are called 'call options' (technically, calls) and 'put options' (technically, puts), and these are traded in large volumes on the market, the options market. The market participants use the options in order to speculate with a small amount of money or to collect risk premiums.

Risk premiums and their dependence on volatility

What is the price of an option? Let's assume we have a call option for share Z (the underlying) at a price of 100 EUR (the strike). If the share is currently at 30 EUR and the option has four weeks to run, the option will be worth almost nothing. Assuming the share price is 130 EUR and the option expires in four weeks, the option will cost at least 30 EUR. If the share is at 85 EUR and the expiration date is in four weeks, the price depends strongly on the volatility of the share.

If the share price does not change significantly for many weeks, it is unlikely that the share price will exceed 100 EUR until the end of the term. Hence, the option is worth only a few cents. However, if the share price fluctuates by 5 EUR per day, everything is possible, and the option is worth several EUR.

The value of the option depends strongly on the volatility, because the higher it is, the more likely it is that the strike price will be reached or even exceeded. Someone hoping the option will not reach the strike is called a writer. The higher the volatility and the higher the probability that the strike will be reached, the higher the premium the writer will receive.

Options are available for most asset classes, provided that the underlying asset can be priced, which is usually the case if the underlying asset is listed on a stock exchange. Only in the case of bonds is it problematic, because only government bonds of industrialised countries, for which futures are also available, are suitable for the options market.

Use as an asset class: opportunities and risks

Options are dangerous for private investors because the risk of loss is unlimited. Private investors can lose house and home. That is why they should leave this instrument to institutional investors only. The same applies to futures. If private investors still want to engage in the market for options, then warrants (as buyers) or discount puts (as writers) are the way to go. These certificates have the same payoff profile as options, but they can be traded as securities. Money has to be paid, but only the invested amount can be lost. A 100% loss hurts, but if on top of the loss further money has to be paid, that is far worse.

As an equity fund holder, you will be invested in options sooner than you can imagine. Many equity fund managers are allowed to use options according to the fund rules, often justifying this so that they can protect themselves in times of crisis. This is basically understandable because an equity fund manager cannot sell all of his shares when the stock market is struggling. He can either hedge with futures or buy put options. When the markets start to crumble, volatility on the stock exchanges increases, and so do option prices. Hedging then becomes very expensive. Once prices stop falling and the markets do not recover, the hedge has cost a lot of money as well as performance and the fund does not participate in a recovery as long as the hedge is still active. So, this scenario hurts in two ways.

Equity funds that act as a writer of call stock options and simultaneously own the underlying stock are called writer funds.

Example: An equity fund has XYZ shares, which are quoted at 100 EUR. The calls, which still have three months to run, are sold at a strike price of 120 EUR. For this, a premium is paid, for example, 5 EUR. Assuming that at the end of the term the share is traded for 119 EUR, the manager has earned the premium as an additional bonus. If the share is quoted at 130 EUR, the manager has to pay 10 EUR because of the option, but his shares have increased by 30 EUR - he still makes a profit of 25 EUR. Without the option (5 EUR premium income and a 10 EUR additional payment) his profit would be 30 EUR.

This strategy protects against unlimited writer loss. The manager has hedged his options (technically covered), could earn 5 EUR additionally, but has limited the profit possibility of his share to 20 EUR.

There are also funds where option strategies are the core of their investment approach. You will recognise these funds if they contain the word 'premium.' However, they can also be found under 'Absolute Return,' 'Market Neutral' or 'Volatility Income.' The price trends here often look impressive until the next stock market crash. At most times, the stock market is calm and option premiums are low. In order to generate sufficient income in the fund, the fund manager has to buy options with a small risk buffer. This pulls him down very quickly in a crash situation. Once the crash is in sight, options with a larger risk buffer that still generate lucrative income can be sold. But volatility does not only double in the downward maelstrom of the markets; it can also increase fivefold. Even a fund manager cannot predict the right time to enter the market. In the case of option strategies, puts with a lower strike are frequently sold, and even lower strikes are bought. This is important in order to eliminate the unlimited risk of loss, but the pressure to permanently deliver performance is enormous. Do you want to be invested in a fund that yields only 1% to 2% for five years when you could have earned 30% to 40% on stocks in the same period? In order to get 5% to 6% every year, there has to be a risk. Unfortunately, this is how it goes.

Potential paths to wealth

———❦❦———

Now that you have an overview of the basics of the stock market, let's put your knowledge into practice. We will work out a wealth roadmap, and in doing this, I will use the technical terms that I have explained in the previous chapter. If they have slipped your mind, you can look up most of them in the glossary at the end of this book.

Before we start, one more note. In this book, I will not recommend specific products, nor will you find links to specific tools. I will also not mention any security identification numbers. This is because I do not want to talk about identification numbers that may no longer exist after the book is published.

The goal

The first thing you should know is what you want to achieve in the stock market. Do you just want to have the thrill and excitement of being active on the stock exchange? What sounds strange and possibly applies to almost everybody who likes to go to a casino (those who do not have a gambling addiction problem) is not so far-fetched. By thrill, I mean the chance to make a lucrative win and the excitement that comes with it. The stock or derivative selection, the shaking, the joy. I don't know about any statistics on why private investors are active in the stock market. Even if there were any statistics based on surveys, I'm not sure if they would paint an accurate picture of the true reasons. Who would admit that he is active on the stock exchange because of greed and dreams of great wealth?

Once, in my early 20s, I went to a casino and lost 100 EUR. I thought about what would have happened if I had invested the money in warrants. It might have cost a 10 EUR order fee, but the chance of a total loss was about 70%, and the probability of a positive return was 20%. The chance to make an enormous profit, like tenfold, was at 10%. Looking at my gambling experience from this angle, I should have rather invested my money in warrants.

Now, before you start searching the Internet for warrants, this goes beyond the basics I want to introduce you to and should not be discussed any further in this publication. My book is aimed at beginners or conservative investors. For the area of certificates or warrants, additional literature is needed.

I will go out on a limb and make the assertion that many private investors want to invest in the stock market because of the potential gains, and that is perfectly fine. But there are also more conservative goals. Someone wants to build up his retirement provision. Another has inherited a large sum of money and would like to put it to work rather than just have it lying in a bank account that does not earn much interest.

Should it be your goal to accumulate a million euroin assets, that is not reprehensible. It only becomes difficult if you want to achieve this in three years and your starting capital is 10,000 EUR (which, by the way, equals a profit of 365% per year). I can write down a roadmap, but it will fail with a probability of 99%, and all your invested capital will most likely be lost.

I would rather show you realistic ways to invest money profitably. In 2020, the average net income in Germany was just under 2,100 EUR per month, and the savings rate was more than 10%. If a 20-year-old manages to invest 210 EUR every month in stocks, he will, according to historical stock returns (approximately 8.5% per year), have accumulated the desired EUR 1 million by his early 60s, assuming that returns will continue to be at least 8.5% on the stock market. If you are just starting out in your 30s, you will need 450 EUR every month to get the same result.

But does the target have to be EUR 1 million? If the 20-year-old saves only 100 EUR a month, he will have 650,000 EUR once he is 67 years old. Let's assume that taxes will take half of that (only a worst-case scenario), and the hard-working saver would have 325,000 EUR net at his disposal in old age. Every month he can withdraw 820 EUR of this amount until his 100th birthday. Currently, the tax on capital gains (in Germany) is 25%. If this does not change, there would be 1,200 EUR left over each month until his 100th birthday.

When creating the roadmap, I will focus on exemplary lower but lucrative targets; however, I will give you the means to tailor the plan to your needs and goals.

Timing of payout

You want to retire at 67, and on the first day of your retirement, you want to push the payout button? Beware! If it happens to be a crash year and the markets lose more than 40% in one year (as was the case in 2001, 2007 or in the spring of 2020 for the DAX®), 500,000 EUR quickly turned into 250,000 EUR. In the past, losses were usually made up completely within a few years, but in the case of the Corona crisis in 2020, the markets recovered only in a few months. As long as you do not aim for an amount X and want to press the payout button immediately when it is reached, you will possibly need a payout phase in addition to the accumulation phase.

There is nothing wrong with defining a goal that includes both. In fact, it may be best. You start the payout phase after 30 years and pay out immediately if an amount X is reached before then. If you need a specific date when the money must be available, you will need an endowment insurance policy. This can guarantee you a sum X at a certain date, but it will yield a much lower return than an investment that you manage yourself.

Amount of the payout

The amount of payout you want depends on how much time you have, what funds you have available each month, and how much security you want to have.

A 20-year-old who wants one hundred percent security and can pay 100 EUR to an endowment policy every month will have about 50,500 EUR after 40 years, assuming the currently guaranteed interest rate of 0.25% (example for Germany). That makes a return of 2,500 EUR. Even if the return will be higher in practice, the security only applies to the first 50 to 500 EUR.

So, think about how much money you really need as a minimum, and do not put all your eggs in one basket. If you have paid off a property at the time of your retirement, you will need less in stock gains. The 20-year-old then needs perhaps only 50 EUR per month to invest because 185,000 EUR in potential equity gains after 40 years will be enough for a comfortable retirement.

The building blocks required to reach the goal.

Once you have defined your goal based on the investment period and available sum, the most difficult disciplines have to be tackled: timing (i.e., the point of entry and exit) and the investment objectives.

Timing

One-time investment

The stock market master André Kostolany suggested buying shares, taking sleeping pills, and waking up again after many years. He certainly did not assume that the money would be invested in only one share, but rather in 10 to 15 different ones, or even better, in a stock index. The individual share carries an enormous risk. Apple, Microsoft, or Amazon were good examples of this in the past. Unfortunately, there are even more examples of how stocks have lost 99% of their value. Investing in 15 stocks in different countries and industries, it is possible that after 30 years, five of them will have gone bankrupt, five will have merged with others (which is not necessarily bad for your investment), and five will have made several 100% price gains. According to the motto, 'On the stock exchange, you can gain 1,000% but you can only lose 100%,' the total investment will most likely be clearly in the plus. If you had 40,000 EUR initial capital, distributed this evenly between 15 shares in 1997 and one share would have been Amazon (closing price in 1997: 4.30 USD), then your portfolio in 2021 would already have been worth 1.8 million USD.

But hand on heart:

1.   Firstly, you have to be lucky enough to have such a treasure in your depot.
2.   You have to be able to hold it for a long time and not suffer a heart attack when the share loses more than 20% of its value due to stock market.

Even without a stroke of luck, this tactic with the investment would probably go well; however, one can increase the probability with a different timing variant and other investment objects.

The savings plan

You may have already heard of the savings plan. Possibly it was the reason you bought this book. With a savings plan, you invest regularly, for example once a month, with a previously determined amount over many years. This comes with an unbeatable advantage: your purchase price (the price at which you bought on average) will never be the highest price of the investment object. The cost price will be significantly below the historical high. That doesn't mean you can't be in the red overalls. If you bought a stock every month for 20 years at an average price of 20 EUR and it peaked at 30 EUR, its price can still fall to a few cents.

If you buy monthly, you buy in weak times just as you do in strong times. No one knows when strong or weak times will begin or end. It would be pure speculation to stop or start a savings plan with a forecast of possible market developments. If stock markets are constantly rising, a one-time investment is better, but the stock market has not turned out to be a one-way street in the past.

Over the years, you will reach an average price, which is not the best in theory but not the worst either. The technical term for this is 'Cost Average Effect.' If you don't have a starting capital and you have to invest every month, you have little choice but to use the savings plan. Every two years, I save money to invest, but finding the right time to invest is entirely dependent on luck.

Investment objects

Besides the timing problem, which can still be mitigated by a long-term investment or a savings plan, making the right choice of investment objects is the most difficult task on the path to wealth. Only one thing is clear: in times without interest, the only asset classes are real estate and stocks or stock indices. Since real estate is a single sector and therefore represents an enormous risk, I will limit myself to equities. Real estate is certainly a possible addition, just as physical gold can be an additional protection in the home safe. But the long-term returns come from investments in companies whose own goal is to generate profits to distribute to shareholders. I will refrain from analysing certificates and ETCs in this book, though, as the issuer risk cannot be ruled out in the long term.

Target funds

Does it make sense to leave one's old-age provision or savings to an equity fund manager?

As an institutional investor, I would certainly do it. I have a manager, I give him rules and a strategy, and if necessary, I will replace him with another manager if the performance is not right. For this, I, as an institutional investor, will never have to pay an issue surcharge or a high manager fee.

As a private investor, you may be able to avoid the issue surcharge via a savings plan, but even that is not guaranteed. If the market's stock return is historically 8.5% per year and you pay 1% manager fees each year, the manager would have to earn 9.5% annually for decades to recoup the fees for you. In reality, however, hardly anyone makes the 8.5%.

If you don't feel able to manage your portfolio with shares or ETFs yourself, you can give your money to a target fund manager. But finding a good fund is even more difficult.

Individual stocks

Putting together a portfolio yourself can be an exciting proposition and can have its advantages. Provided it is well diversified, i.e., each position has a total weight of only 5% to 10% at the beginning, the risk that comes with this strategy is moderate. Selecting stocks that you may want to hold for decades can take days. Of course, you can choose your stocks randomly, it is not said that you will be less successful. Try typing the following into a search engine: 'monkey with a dart.' However, if your random selection only includes stocks from one country or a single industry in your portfolio, the risk increases significantly.

If you are making individual investments, you will need start-up capital. A stock position at the beginning should be between 1,000 and 3,000 EUR since you have to expect order fees of 15 to 75 EUR (depending on the bank and stock exchange). Investing only 400 EUR with an order fee of 25 EUR, you start with a loss of over 6%.

For a reasonable level of diversification, you will need 40,000 to 50,000 EUR. If you do not have this money you will have to save for a long time before being able to invest for the first time. During this time, your money will not have generated any returns.

ETFs

For years, consumer advisors, financial experts, and old stock market hands have agreed about one thing: A savings plan with ETFs is the best way to build up your wealth accumulation. They often point out the following reasons:

ETFs (European Regulation) Pros:
- Track the market, and hardly any fund manager succeeds in managing to beat the market on a sustained basis. The conclusion is that investing in the market is the best way to go.

- Are more favourable in their annual management fee than actively managed funds. The purchase via savings plans is sometimes even free of charge.

- If the fund company becomes insolvent, the assets are protected, and the investor is entitled to them.

- Do not require tonnes of money and are therefore suitable for every purse.

Let me give you my two cents on this: I can underline most of it but the term 'market' has to be seen critically in this context. You now have hundreds of ETFs to choose from, and not all of them track a diversified stock market. There are ETFs that only go up when stocks go down; some track bond indices; some track commodities. In addition, there are ETFs on individual sectors, some with sustainability filters, and some that describe themselves as 'optimised.' Each ETF has different opportunities and risks. How is the beginner supposed to set up the right savings plan strategy?

There is some skepticism in the media with regards to ETFs:

'The ETF also buys the obviously bad stocks because they are in the index that it tracks.'

'Many markets that the ETF tracks have foreign currency risk.'

'The ETF cannot protect itself against stock market crashes.'

'We are in an ETF bubble; if the markets fall, the ETFs must inevitably have to sell as well, causing stock prices to plunge even harder.'

Note from me: As far as one can tell what bad stocks are, the first point is correct. However badly performing stocks usually have a very low weighting in an index and therefore also in the ETF. An active manager can only protect his fund if he correctly foresees the crisis (which is difficult, maybe impossible), and if he has succeeded in doing so, he also needs to correctly predict the end of the crisis in order to unwind his hedge. The foreign currency risk is real; we could, however, reduce it by mixing different markets. I'll come to that later.

I see ETFs as the best way to build wealth. Even if there is enough initial capital, I would still consider a self-built stock portfolio to hold as an admixture to the ETF portfolio. This would also be my preferred strategy as a fund manager, while on the institutional side, I would use futures instead of ETFs.

What can happen during the investment phase

Specific equity events.
During the asset accumulation phase, you can usually only put your feet up if you have made a one-time investment in equities. Nevertheless, every now and then you might receive mail.

Annual general meetings

Once a year, you will receive a notice of a meeting for all shares. You can accept them, but you do not have to. If the meeting were to be held in Tokyo, it would be quite a trip.

Recently, such meetings have been held online, thus avoiding travel costs.

Stock splits

If shares are rising and seeming to be expensive, corporations like to adjust that by applying the tool of stock splits. An example: Initially, 10 million shares have been issued, and if the company gives one bonus share for each share held by each shareholder, the company will end up with 20 million shares. This move in turn leads to a halving of the share price, which is the intended result. Your share, which was worth 400 EUR, is now worth only 200 EUR. However, you now hold twice as many shares in your securities account, and you have not incurred a loss. Stock corporations do this because shares that cost 200 EUR are more likely to be bought than shares that cost 400 EUR, and it also helps distribute the available funds in a better way. Sticking with the example above, if someone has 1,000 EUR at his disposal, he can now invest fully in five shares. Before, it would have been a maximum of two shares and only 800 EUR.

Capital increases

Another tool a corporation can use is a capital increase. The company issues rights for new shares, but these are not free of charge. In this case, you have to buy the shares when you exercise the subscription rights. This means further investment. You don't have to exercise the subscription rights or have them sold via your bank if they have value. As a rule, you will receive mail in which everything should be explained in an understandable way.

Severance offers, mergers

If shares are held for a long period of time, other things can happen. To explain them all would go beyond the scope of this book. However, it can happen that someone makes you a lucrative offer (a takeover bid) for your shares. It could be that shares are forcibly sold because someone has almost all the shares of the company and, to exaggerate, only yours are still missing and the company is to be taken off the stock exchange. Whatever comes your way, your bank is obligated to explain everything to you by mail in an understandable way. In the event of a compulsory squeeze-out, you have the right to withdraw from the company and will receive the money for your shares, hence, no longer be invested in it.

Specific fund events

If you have ETFs or target funds, you do not need to deal with corporate actions. There are other events that can happen, though.

Fund closures or mergers

Target-date funds can be liquidated, either because all investors have redeemed their units or because the administering management company terminates the fund without another company taking it over. Sometimes funds merge. Most often, this happens when a target fund has performed poorly in the past and no one wants to buy it anymore. It also might have become too small. In the event of a closure, you will receive the last share price if you have not sold beforehand.

Tip: In the event of closure, do not remain invested in the fund until the last day. Your bank will inform you in advance about the liquidation. In the last days of its life, the fund will make many sales and incur costs, which will negatively affect the fund price, so you are indirectly paying for the fees of the liquidation.

ETFs can also close down, for example, if the index can no longer be tracked or the fund has become too small. In this case, you also receive the fund assets paid out proportionately.

Suspension of the return of unit certificate transactions

Should a fund have massive cash outflows and not be able to service them through the sale of its assets, share certificate transactions may be suspended. In the past, this was often the case with real estate funds or other funds, which in turn were invested in real estate funds. However, even an equity fund that is 100% invested in equities can run into problems. If the fund is invested in small companies (technically 'small caps'), it can take days or even weeks to sell its assets in a market-friendly way. Then you certainly do not have to wait for months or years as you would with a real estate fund, but if you need money the day after tomorrow, this can be annoying.

Change of fees in your securities account

Before you decided which bank should manage your securities account, you probably compared prices. You may have selected certain ETFs because they were available free of charge through a savings plan. Sometimes something was free, but in the fine print it said that it was free only for a certain time. The basic fees for the securities account do not change quietly; you will be informed about that. Individual products which may have been on offer for a certain period of time may change. If you then pay a 1.5% order fee on a savings plan for 20 years, which another bank offers free of charge, it can really make a difference. It might also happen that a target fund has no front-end surcharge for a while and then suddenly this is changed again.

Tip: Take a look at the statements at least once a year to check whether the fees are still as you expected them to be and whether a competitor bank has a better offer. If the competing bank is better, switch! It's easier than moving an account, and most of the time, the receiving bank will give you a reward. However, it may be the case that the new bank does not offer the same funds; you should check that beforehand. In general, it can be said that the largest and most important ETFs are usually offered by all providers.

Change in income and expenditure situation

Throughout life, many things happen outside of the deposit account. Marriage, house purchase, children, divorce, job loss, inheritance, and so on. Some events justify an increase in the investment rate, some a decrease. Some things cause a premature termination of the savings phase or a payout from the assets.

A savings plan does not cause fixed costs. You can increase it, stop it for a short time, or make it dynamic (deposits are increased by a certain percentage each year). If you need money from the investment assets, you may incur losses, especially in the early years. Try to avoid such a situation by always keeping a cash reserve, even if it does not earn any interest.

If perhaps your wealth goal is reached much sooner than you thought, do not be afraid to take your first profits through partial sales. Then you cushion the risk that the stock market plays a trick on you on your planned payout date.

The psychology

The stock market is a mind game. Understatements, exaggerations, greed, profits, and losses. When you take out endowment insurance or a private pension, you will not experience all these feelings and fluctuations. The fund managers behind the scenes expose themselves to this pressure. When investing in a target fund, you will not be as affected by that as the fund manager is.

If you have a savings plan, you will be more in touch with the game. After the initial execution, you may check on the performance on a daily basis. Rationally, that does not make any sense, even if after one week there is 5% plus or minus. Assuming your saving phase is 30 years, after one month you will have paid in just 0.0027% of the investment amount. But the thrill is there, and that's okay. At some point, you get used to it and only look at the portfolio once a month or twice a year. It's best if you don't look in there that often; otherwise, you will be annoyed if you were just at 150,000 EUR in the plus and shortly after that, you only see a profit of 50,000 EUR because the stock markets are currently affected by some crisis. This could possibly lead you to start thinking about selling everything quickly and securing the 50,000 EUR. The stock exchange is relentless in this matter; whoever secures the 50,000 EUR, may be angry three years later because the profit would have been 300,000 EUR. Many then jump on the train again and ruin their life's work because the cost price was spoiled. As I said before, the stock market is merciless.

With individual shares, the psychological effect can be far worse, and being attached to certain shares can be dangerous. A time might come when these shares should be sold, but it does not happen because of the investor's loyalty. Even those who are emotionally stable, the ones who set a target date for selling in the distant future and really stuck to it, could experience this. He was once a millionaire, but now he is far from being one because the sale was made too late. That is hard to digest.

If you choose the individual shares and a share has ensured that your investment goal has already been reached after less than half of the planned investment time, take the profits and don't let greed get the best of you. It's easier said than done, but I must warn you about the psychology trap. This is, by the way, where the target fund has an advantage. The fund manager is less emotionally attached to the investments because it is not his money and can therefore make better decisions. But he has a problem when things don't go so well. As a private individual, you are not accountable to anyone and can better endure such phases.

The roadmap

Now it's time for me to get specific. Since I cannot recommend individual stocks (thin ice), I will show examples of possible savings plans with ETFs.

Financial calculator

To start with, we need the investment amounts that you can raise today or in the future. For this, you can use a financial calculator, which can be found free of charge on the Internet. Where to find them: look for it in the search machine.

Set one-time amount and savings rate

In addition to the investment amounts, you could also set the final amount and see how much you have to invest and for how long. But be careful! If you invest in assets with price fluctuations, which is almost always the case, the calculated data is subject to enormous uncertainty. It can happen that shares fall by 50% from January to December in one year. As long as you had not invested the complete amount on December 31 of the previous year, you would not be 50% in the red. If you have been saving monthly for 20 or 30 years before that, your price is so low that you may not even be in the loss area at all. However, after a crash, the value of your total investment is lower than you might have calculated for day X, so don't plan on using a certain amount of money on a certain day to pay off the rest of your real estate loan.

Excursus: It happened that the bank that issued a real estate loan offered to put money into a group-owned investment fund instead of paying monthly installments. Since this would supposedly increase more in the long term than the interest payments, the real estate loan could be paid off before the planned final maturity date. If this happened to be a target fund, a markup of 4% to 5% an annual management fee of 1%, and if that wasn't enough, a deposit fee for the securities account itself would gladly be taken by the bank for their services. If, on top of that, the fund manager missed the average stock performance of the market, disaster was complete. Madness! The bank gained a lot of money without any risk, and the real estate loan as well as the interest still have to be paid in full by the customer. Such financing models are offered with ETFs and without deposit fees. This is certainly much better in terms of fees, but the risk of not having the required sum on day X is still borne by you!

The better way is to enter a starting capital and a savings rate. If you do not have a starting capital, enter 0. Should you not want a savings plan, you can leave the savings rate blank. Often the savings rate can be kept dynamic, i.e., add an increase rate if you wish to do so.

Set fees and interest rate

You can enter charges, but you don't have to, because you can also simply deduct them from the interest rate. Concerning the interest rate, you are requested to put in the average annual yield. Here you can enter 8% for a stock investment. No one knows whether shares will really yield this return in the next 20, 30, or 50 years. Statistically, this return is even higher, but it must be adjusted for inflation and other uncertainties.

If you invest in equity ETFs, the fees are between 0.1% and 0.5% per year. In case you prefer a more conservative approach, let's say 7%, that's just as okay as a more speculative 9%. The calculator is not a promise of return, but it will show you the results with the appropriate deposits and assumed returns. For results without a monthly savings rate, the calculator is more reliable. With monthly savings rates, there is more uncertainty since no theoretical model can express how many weak and strong stock market months are on the way. Historically, for most indices, the pure savings plan was weaker.

Sample calculations with hypothetical returns:
Note that this sample does not consider any tax deduction.
Initial capital only:

Starting capital	20,000 EUR
Savings rate (monthly)	0
Annual interest (less fees)	8%
Run-time (in years)	20
Outcome	93,219.14 EUR

Saving rate only:

Starting capital	0
Savings rate (monthly)	250 EUR
Annual interest (less fees)	8%
Run-time (in years)	25
Outcome	228,821.59 EUR

Initial capital only:

Starting capital	2,000 EUR
Savings rate (monthly)	150 EUR
Annual interest (less fees)	7%
Run-time (in years)	36
Outcome	301,055.46 EUR

If you can save 500 EUR monthly at the age of 32, you could also retire as a millionaire, even following a more conservative approach. That is, if the returns on stocks remain at their historic level in the future. As already mentioned, the calculation does not include any taxation.

Starting capital	0
Savings rate (monthly)	500 EUR
Annual interest (less fees)	7.70%
Run-time (in years)	35
Outcome	1,007,648.4 EUR

Selection of securities

The supreme discipline is diversification, i.e., the broad spread of risk in order not to get caught up in a single economic problem of a country, as happened in the past in Japan, Russia, or Greece. I can only warn against trusting the DAX® alone just because it is an index with solid German stocks. A lot can happen in a period of 30 or 40 years, even in Germany.

Possible risks exemplified by popular indices:
MSCI World

- Covers all industrialised countries, mostly the USA.

- In addition to the strong dependence on the USA, there is also a currency (dollar) risk.

MSCI All Countries World

- Emerging markets are included.

- The USA is still strongly represented, and the dollar risk is unabatedly high.

Eurostoxx 50 or Stoxx 600

- Represents Europe.

- If Italy, Spain, or Portugal wobble because of their high debt, it pulls the index down, even if France or Germany are solid.

However, risk can also be an opportunity. Stocking the entire portfolio only with European securities, in order to avoid the dollar inevitably leads to a euro risk. A country with high interest rates usually has a stronger currency, but this currency also makes exports more expensive for the respective economy.

There is nothing wrong with investing 50% in ETFs with a focus outside of Europe. Sectors, individual countries, or special themes should make up a maximum of 20% of the portfolio. If you have a savings rate of 150 EUR, you can usually divide it into six ETFs with a common minimum rate of 25 EUR.

Examples of balanced savings plans:

150 EUR:
Six ETFs of 25 EUR each are spread worldwide to cover the USA, Asia, Europe, Germany, Technology, and Small Caps (small companies).

250 EUR:
Two ETFs at 50 EUR are distributed between Europe and the rest of the world. Six ETFs at 25 EUR distributed among Asia: technology 1 (e.g., water), technology 2 (e.g., artificial intelligence), sector 1 (e.g., healthcare), sector 2 (e.g., batteries), and mid-sized companies.

If the possible savings rates are smaller, then they can be split in half between Europe and the rest of the world, as most of the sectors are also in the major indices. Putting everything on one or two industries, technologies, or countries would not be a balanced strategy. Whilst this can generate long-term returns of 15% or more, it also comes with an increased risk.

What to do with the one-time investment

It may be the case that you have a starting capital at your disposal or expect larger one-time payments at regular intervals (bonuses, commissions) that you expect to invest.

Scenario 1:

If the one-time investment is in relation to what will come over, the savings rate will be very low.

1. You invest this right at the beginning, divided into two or several ETFs. If you save for 20 or 30 years, the rate you get now has no impact.

2. You save money and increase your savings rate at times when you are annoyed by price losses or when the tabloid news is talking about a stock crash. Once the one-time sum is fully invested, you reduce the savings rate back to its normal level. With this strategy, you are not annoyed about losses but are finally happy to be able to invest the money, and you may even beat the return of the market, which hardly any fund manager achieves.

Scenario 2:

The sum you have at your disposal is very high, or you plan not to set up a savings plan at all. No one knows if the stock market is on its way to new highs or if it is about to tip. Therefore, the investment may achieve the desired return after 30 years; however, you may also experience losses for six years and curse the market. It is better to spread a large sum over at least nine to ten years with a savings plan; then you will have invested in good and bad times.

Scenario 3:

You are a retiree and have received a one-time sum (e.g., at retirement).

It is the simplest case. As long as you do not want to invest the money for your heirs to inherit, keep your hands off the stock market. Rather look for savings opportunities in everyday life than for investment opportunities.

If you still have a loan somewhere, pay it off early. If you have a way to save an extra 25 EUR a month, that equals 300 EUR per year. In 2021, you would have to invest 150,000 EUR overnight to get 300 EUR interest per year. Probably no bank would have accepted such a sum, but it shows what you can do as a pensioner to avoid financial difficulties.

Which bank to choose to set up the roadmap

Have you decided what your roadmap should look like? Then, finally, you can think about which bank is best suited for the plan. If you plan to make monthly savings in ETFs, see which banks offer that for free. Sometimes banks only offer this for proprietary products free of charge, in which case you need to check at the very beginning whether your investment ideas can be implemented by the bank.

Invest in shares and buy them regularly. Also look for the broker fees. These should be a maximum of 1 to 1.5% of your expected order size, not more than 15 EUR for an order size of 1,000 EUR. If you are planning to buy shares only once and leave them in the securities account for years, you can let your bank do this for an order fee of 60 EUR. But make sure that your securities account does not incur additional fees per month, because that will be expensive over the years.

Of course, I can understand if you want to have a bank advisor look over your schedule, and you might also want to be looked after on an ongoing basis if you are prepared to pay the high fees that come with that service. With my book, I have equipped you with the basics of the stock exchange, and I have given you the tools you need to act confidently and smartly in your dealings with your advisor. Likewise, you have the tools to control, expand, or improve your portfolio.

Important remarks at the end

In this book, we have gone through the financial market. You should now be able to open a securities account, know what shares are, what to expect as a shareholder, and also have an overview of bonds and commodities. We looked closer at the topic of investment funds, as this is usually the first investment opportunity. There are several books on the subject of savings plans and ETFs on the market. What you could read in my last chapter of this book is basically exactly what you will find in this literature. But that is also part of the basics of the stock market.

I have familiarised you with the most important terms. If a trader in a pub in London's financial district asks his colleague, 'We have to short the commodities; the backwardation is very pronounced. Do you know of a counterparty who will reliably perform and cheaply?' then you now know that the one wants to bet on falling commodities because the future contracts are much cheaper than today's. Now he is looking for a partner who will make a contract with him in which they agree on exactly this and ask the other for a tip. Exciting, isn't it?

I've called for caution more than once in the book. In conclusion, I want to warn you about an expensive experience but discourage you from it at all costs. If you want to deepen your knowledge using internet search engines or financial websites, sometimes you will be shown advertisements that may lead you to scammers. This happens especially when you type in the names of stocks that have recently gone through a very rapid price development. Suspect number one for some time now has been bitcoin, something that I have deliberately left out of this book because this is not part of the basics of the stock market. Even with a stock search via the search engine, this can happen to you. The advertising algorithms know exactly which ads are clicked on; after all, many people dream of becoming rich quickly at some point in their lives.

Even if there is no fraud behind it and you are being recruited to invest in medium-sized bonds or equity investments, keep one thing in mind: If the investment is really as great as the glossy brochures promise, advertising would not be necessary as institutional investors would buy them anyway.

No one in the financial market has a crystal ball in which tomorrow's prices are visible, and good products don't need advertising. Keep this warning in mind if anyone tries to sell you something.

What belongs in the big picture of the stock market? Trading leveraged products, certificates, or CFDs. Analysis of shares or markets, chart analysis, short-term trading ideas. For each of these topics, there are additional books and specialists.
If you enjoyed this book, please leave a fair rating.

I will close with stock market wisdom that I very often have in mind when I buy something on the financial market and which comes from André Kostolany: 'Never run after a streetcar, nor an investment; the next one is sure to come.'

Glossary

ABS: security that is secured by other receivables (e.g., credit card debts, consumer loans).

Absolute return: strategy to make profits at any market phase

Asset allocation: distribution of assets to specific assets (e.g., 30% cash, 50% stocks, 20% real estate)

Asset classes: classification of assets (e.g., stocks, real estate)

Asset manager: person who decides which assets are purchased

Asset: asset (e.g., Daimler share, SAP bond)

Backwardation: rising futures prices as final maturity approaches

Baisse: longer period of falling prices

Bearish: a market in a negative mood

Benchmark: a level or result used for comparison

best/cheapest: sell as expensively as possible or buy as cheaply as possible

Bull market: prolonged period of rising prices

Callable: a bond that can be terminated by the issuer

Capital management companies: companies that set up and administer funds

Certificates: bearer bonds whose conditions depend on certain market events

Collateral Agreement: contract on collateral to be provided,

Contango: falling futures prices, the closer to final maturity

Cost Average Effect: through regular buying, an average cost price is created that is below the highest prices

Custodian: a custodian bank for a fund

Derivatives: financial products whose value is derived from the prices of other products

Disclosure Ordinance: obligation to provide information on sustainability approaches

Discount put: a certificate that benefits from falling or, at most, slightly rising prices but becomes worthless if prices rise too much

Diversification: spreading of risk

Dividends: cash payments from companies to their shareholders

ESG: criteria for sustainable investment

EUR hedged: a product that is hedged against currency losses from a euro perspective

Fair value: true value of a company if all the information for assessing it is publicly available

Fixed-interest bond: a bond that pays a fixed interest rate at regular intervals

Floater: a bond that has a variable interest rate

Forward curves: the price development of a future at the end of its term

Fund of funds: fund that invests in other funds

Futures: a standardised agreement to deliver an item of a specified quality at a specified time

Growth: stocks that promise great performance

Hedge funds: funds with alternative investment strategies that can make a profit at any time

Issuer risk: the risk that the issuer will become insolvent

Leverage: factor by which a derivative increases if the underlying asset rises by 1%

Limit down: futures that are suspended from trading because the market falls too much

Limit up: futures that are suspended from trading because the market is rising too much

Long: bet on rising prices

Market capitalisation: the number of shares issued by a company multiplied by the current share price

market: buy at cheap or sell at best

MBS: security backed by real estate loans

Options: agreement to buy (call) or sell (put) something at a certain price at a certain time

Order fee: purchase or sale fee

Order: purchase or sale order

Outperformance: better result than the standard

Performance: result (can be positive or negative) Security that is secured against default by something of value

Physically replicated: an index that has been exactly replicated with the values it contains

Portfolio: the sum of all assets

Primary market: the issuing of shares or bonds by a company

Purchase price: the price at which the average share was purchased

Rating agencies: companies that assess the creditworthiness of other companies

Rating: credit rating of a company, according to school grades

Reset: compensation for profits and losses

Risk premiums: money paid to sell an option, with the risk that the option must be realised

Rolls: replacing an expiring future with one that has a longer maturity

Secondary market: an exchange

Short Selling: selling a product that one does not possess with the aim of buying it back at a lower price

Short: betting on falling prices

SRI: strategy of investing with sustainability

Stock picking: selecting stocks that have the potential to outperform the market

Swaps: the exchange of the performance of one product by two partners

Timing: timing of the purchase or sale

Total Return Index: index where the returns are reinvested

Total Return: an attempt is made to generate the return from several asset classes

Trading: short-term buying and selling

UCITS: a mutual fund, with certain investor protection rules

UCITS: mutual funds with certain EU investor protection rules

Value: a selection of stocks whose price is below their fair value

Warrant: like options, but packaged as a security that can lose a maximum of 100% of its value

Zero bonds: bonds without interest, creditors are compensated by rising prices

Calculation and data sources

All data retrieved on 09/10/2021.

Historical share price and dividend data, Intershop and Allianz shares:

https://www.finanzen.net/historische-kurse/intershop

https://www.boerse.de/historische-kurse/AllianzAktie/DE0008404005

https://www.boerse.de/dividenden/Allianz/DE0008404005

Yield calculations for savings plans:

https://www.zinsen-berechnen.de/sparrechner.php

BMW sample bond from the bond chapter:

ISIN XS2280845145

https://www.boerse-stuttgart.de/dede/tools/produktsuche/anleihen-finder/

Scientific Beta Japan HFI Multi-Beta Multi-Strategy Six Factor EW

Market Beta Adjusted

https://www.onvista.de/etf/SCIBETA-HFE-JAPAN-EQUITY-6F-EWUCITS-ETF-EUR-ACC-ETF-IE00BDBRDY56

Average net earnings Germany 2020:

https://de.statista.com/statistik/daten/studie/370558/umfrage/monatliche-nettoloehne-und-gehaelter-je-arbeitnehmer-in-deutschland/

Disclaimer

I have written this book to the best of my knowledge and belief. It is based on the fundamentals of my education, my daily work in portfolio management, and my experience. If I have an opinion about something, it can be wrong, which is why I have tried to write it in the subjunctive.

I deliberately have not given any recommendations for a specific investment. However, I have pointed out what risk diversification looks like and given you my experience with poorly performing financial market products over the last few years. The return expectations of shares are based on long-term historical data. No one knows if the same returns will be possible in the future or if better or worse results will be achieved.

I have used terms from this book, especially those in the glossary, in my own words and not copied from other sources. This carries the risk that it may not always be scientifically one hundred percent correct, but it is authentic.
I have also restrained myself with making references to websites. Where it has happened, I cannot be held responsible for their content.

I cannot be held responsible for any investments you make after reading this book. I hope that you will not experience any unpleasant surprises in the world of finance and that the book may save you from one or another stumbling block.

Printed in Great Britain
by Amazon